# a load of old ball crunchers

# a load of old ball crunchers

## women in history

### by

## jo brand

SIMON & SCHUSTER
A VIACOM COMPANY

First published in Great Britain by Simon & Schuster Ltd, 1996
A Viacom Company

Simon & Schuster
West Garden Place
Kendal Street
London W2 2AQ

Simon & Schuster of Australia Pty Ltd
Sydney

A CIP catalogue record for this book is available
from the British Library.

0-684816954

Design, Typesetting and Repro
by The Imaging Business

Typographic Design
by Aniz Damani

Printed and bound in Great Britain
by The Baht Press

# contents

# introduction

This book attempts to give you some idea of the lives of fifty women who have in some way made their mark on the world. The further back one goes in history, the harder it gets for women to be noticed, because before the railing chaining efforts of the suffragettes women weren't even considered intelligent enough to put a cross on a bit of paper. Things haven't changed that much since then. Even though we women are supposed to have equality and all that old balls we're still expected to be as decorative as we can, despite the fact that some of us actually like slopping around in something resembling an old sack with curry all over it. Every time I hear some smooth voice-over on a hair advertisement say, 'It's really important to have healthy shiny hair', I think, not if you look like the back of a bus it ain't.

In the age of the supermodel, it's easy to forget that women can manage to do a bit more than totter up and down, wearing expensive clothes and being escorted by some of the less intellectually able Hollywood males. I always like to compare models to supermodels in the way I compare Tampax to Super Tampax: supermodels cost a bit more and they are a lot thicker.

A lot of the women in this book were inspiring to me but some of them are slightly sad types, trapped in the eyes of men by their big chests and pretty faces. I've been trapped by my big chest many a time, but that's unpredictable lifts for you.

My mum was a bit of an inspiration for this book too. She taught me it was better to have and be a good laugh than to be fancied by all the boys in the class. When I was fourteen she said to me, 'All men are bastards, never get married'. A handy piece of advice to carry round, but not a great hit in my O' level English paper. If there are any men reading this, I accept that her statement was a bit over the top, but if you're upset or outraged by it, you probably are a bastard.

When I was a kid, I wasn't sure what I wanted to be when I grew up and no one told me that if I grew out quite a bit, too, I would become a fashion leper, object of lorry drivers' abuse and forever a bridesmaid. This isn't too bad, though, because while the other desperate spinsters are killing and maiming each other to catch the bouquet, I'm on my way to the reception for an early plate of sausage rolls and vol-au-vents. Most of the women in this book did not settle down and marry happily and a good job too or we'd never have heard of them.

In this day and age, of course, it is easier to have a husband, kids, a fulfilling career and make your mark on the world. Sadly, though, you will make your mark on the world as The Most Knackered Woman In The History Of The Known Universe. Feminism appears to have set us free to have a career and do the rest of the bloody work as well. I haven't made up my mind about children yet, but if I do have a baby, I will have a home birth. Not for any romantic reasons, just because I can't be arsed to get off the settee. We women, of course, are still the only sex privileged enough to give birth. They say men can never experience the pain of childbirth . . . they can if you hit them in the goolies with a cricket bat . . . for fourteen hours.

Speaking of men, I would like to thank Jez for all his help in researching this book and for saying, 'They're much more interesting than the men, aren't they?'. I would like to thank Jim, too, for the work he did. And, finally, I'd like to thank my mum, even though I've already mentioned her, for being an amazing person and for going over the garden fence like Sally Gunnell when I was about seven in an attempt to get our pet hare back. Thank God, though, she never encouraged me to become a champion hurdler. I need a trolley to get to the fridge in the mornings. As ever, I'd like to say I hope you enjoy reading this as much as I enjoyed writing it, but after a lot of time in front of the word processor, I look like The Bride Of Frankenstein and feel like a wet teatowel. Not that I'd know what a teatowel feels like. I hate bloody wiping up.

I hope you enjoy it.

# roseanne barr

I once saw a review comparing myself to Roseanne Barr in which we were charmingly referred to as 'the two fat ladies'. And that, as far as the reviewer (male, no doubt) was concerned, was that. However, there are a few differences between us which merit a mention.

*'Sucks to you Liz Taylor, look at the size of this baby'*

Firstly, Roseanne is American and by the rules of comedy each continent is allowed only one fat female comedian. (Dawn French is in a different category from me because she is in a double act.) Roseanne is also different because she is Jewish (I'm a lapsed something or other Church of Englandish type) and was immediately, as a child, presented with a cultural clash because she was brought up in Salt Lake City, Utah, home of the Mormons. No doubt she was driven to comedy by constant Osmonds on the radio. She relates that as a baby she would scream all the time and try and shove her whole fist in her mouth, which would have fitted her well for a career as a screeching whole-baked-potato swallower, if indeed that was a career. (I certainly would have gone for that instead of nursing.)

# a load of old ball crunchers

Roseanne's childhood consisted of Barbie dolls and bikes. Her favourite food was chicken fat, so she was destined to become more of a Lardie doll herself. Being the only Jew at her school it was a bit

*After the success of* **The Partridge Family,** *remaking 60s TV shows is all the rage. This is a shot from MGM's forthcoming* **Joe and Mom 90**

of a surprise when her mother converted to the Mormon religion. No, she wasn't over-impressed by Little Jimmy's 'Long Haired Lover From Liverpool'; a Mormon priest healed Roseanne's paralysed face after she fell. (Roseanne later discovered that it was probably Bell's Palsy, which gets better after forty-eight hours anyway.) A bit of a pity Mrs Barr didn't ask a passing squirrel to cure her daughter, as that would have

been a far more impressive miracle and she would have had to convert to The Tufty Club.

Roseanne is of the opinion that most stand-up comics are emotionally disturbed in some way and so she devoured books on all aspects of the psyche; perfectly reasonable, as books aren't on the list of Weightwatchers forbidden food. She says that, career wise, the only options open to her at school were secretary, mother or teacher, all of which tend to involve being abused by children. (Well, many bosses are puerile and seem to be unable to do very simple things for themselves.) Roseanne by-passed some of those difficult decisions about her future by being hit by a car at the age of sixteen and 'going weird'. She became unable to focus on things or to 'do math'. By the looks of it her spelling got pretty ropey too. She also began to write weird poetry and got an obsession with the number five. (She remarks that many comics are obsessed with numbers. Number twos, yes. Owing to the acute stresses of the work, most comics' bowels function less efficiently than the English end of the Channel Tunnel.)

# 'She was booked on to *The Tonight Show*, which is called that so that Americans can remember when it's on'

To continue down the anal road, Rosanne then went on to do a series of shitty jobs and started having a relationship with someone called Bill. She hitch-hiked all over America and then went back to Bill when she was ill. Despite the fact that she had a temperature of 104, she and Bill still indulged in a spot of 'how's your father'. Blokes are so sympathetic when you're ill aren't they? There you are in the bed wilting pathetically like a consumptive Brontë and in he comes, thinking, 'Well she's in bed, I might as well' and jumps in. The only consolation is

*The assembled crowd, including Roseanne, applaud riotously as some old bloke describes his last bowel movement*

that he'll catch whatever you've got and lie moaning and whinging in agony for days and leave you alone.

# a load of old ball crunchers

Rosanne married Bill and they had three kids, conceived no doubt during bouts of life-threatening illness. At this point she was thin and had a career as a buyer in the clothing industry. Sounds boring doesn't it? Not the clothing industry, being thin I mean.

Roseanne couldn't make up her mind between serious feminist writing (which this is not) and comedy (which hopefully this is). She went in for a talent contest, which she won, and from that was booked on to *The Tonight Show*, which is called that so that Americans can remember when it's on. She never really did her time in the clubs. She says it would have killed me. Well I did it and it didn't kill me. Just maimed me badly.

## 'I'd rather spend her money force-feeding supermodels with chocolate éclairs and keeping them tied up so they couldn't exercise'

Most of us know what happened after this period. Roseanne married Tom Arnold and went on to star in the very successful sitcom *Roseanne*. She also decided that she didn't want to look fat and frumpy any more and went for that plastic surgery business that so many women do, ending up on the front page of a popular American magazine dressed in a basque and all that underwear that women think men love. Men love any underwear that's easy to get off I think is nearer to the truth. I think it's a real shame Roseanne has deserted the 'Come As You Are' brigade and let some surgeon loose on her. Hordes of women all over the world were just getting used to the fact that they had a role model who wasn't obsessed with her appearance and the old girl suddenly has half of her flab chopped off. I'd rather spend her money force-feeding supermodels with chocolate éclairs and keeping them tied up so they couldn't exercise. Much easier to make them look like you than try and look like them . . .

Roseanne is currently engaged in a bitter dispute with Tom Arnold who wants loads of her dosh. She'd have been better off marrying her screen husband in Roseanne. The one and only drawback about him is that she might get to the fridge in the middle of the night and find he's hoovered the entire lot.

# catherine the great

catherine the great didn't become 'great' until fairly late on in life. She started life as plain Sophie the Nothing. She was the daughter of the Prince of Anhalt Zerbst, which was a part of present-day Germany, but in those days princes were ten a penny, so she wasn't pursued by the tabloids in the way she would have been today.

*'My, what an enormous obelisk you've planted in my undergrowth.' (From Carry On Up The Volga, 1971)*

Sophie was instructed as a child by an over-zealous religious teacher and consequently was easily frightened. If only her enemies had realised that later in life they could just creep up and say 'Boo!' things might have been very different. During her childhood, Sophie had a bad accident and fell causing her spine to zigzag and her shoulders to become uneven. Medicine in those days wasn't too sophisticated and the only available man for the job appeared to be the local executioner. Using him was kept secret. Obviously it didn't look good inviting some huge ape dressed in leather and wielding an axe up to the castle to sort out your little girl's spine, although I'm sure some of the new health trusts would do it if they could get away with it.

However, the executioner it was, and he recommended a very uncomfortable back brace in conjunction with a poultice made of virgin's spittle on Catherine's back. (Eat your heart out Deep Heat.) Funnily enough it worked. Just goes to show, you can't beat a bit of virgin's spittle.

# 'Catherine was talked into the marriage. Perhaps she was hoping with all those negative credentials Peter might be a bit of a whizz in the sack'

At the age of fourteen Catherine was invited to Russia with a view to being betrothed to her cousin Karl Ulrich who was to become the Grand Duke Peter. Travelling in those days wasn't what it is now and Catherine arrived in Russia with frostbite and big red blotches all over her face. Come to think of it, I was stuck on an Intercity 125 once with no heating and I had red blotches on my face . . . I'd been crying because the buffet had run out of those chocolate chip cookies the size of dinner plates. Karl Ulrich turned out to be a drunken, selfish idiot who had temper tantrums, par for the course for a future ruler in those days considering the genes in royal families were distributed around the absolute minimum of relatives. Catherine was talked into the marriage. Perhaps she was hoping with all those negative credentials Peter might be a bit of a whizz in the sack.

Catherine got on well with her future auntie-in-law, Empress Elizabeth. Although Peter was a berk, he was a friendly one at first, but once he was sure he was going to marry Catherine he became antagonistic towards her. He was told by his valet he should keep his wife in constant

# a load of old ball crunchers

fear and beat her. No wonder these valets only clean sweet papers out of your car these days, the bastards. It wasn't just the valets in Russia who thought this way though, women had a terrible time. They were kept in 'terrems', confined to the upper floors of Russian houses, and

many women died under punishment from their husbands which was perfectly acceptable then. However, if a woman had the nerve to fight back and bump off her brutish husband, she was buried alive and left to die of thirst. (And people wonder why women bothered to have a feminist movement.)

Peter then got smallpox, as if he needed anything else to make him even less attractive, and he appeared back at court looking hideous and disfigured. On seeing him, Catherine remarked that her 'blood ran cold'. Maybe she should have siphoned some off and got an

*Catherine was always a bit of an embarrassment on tranny night at Madame JoJo's*

executioner to rub it on his face. Thankfully, Peter was so pissed on their wedding night he fell asleep. Face down, one hopes. Peter was really just a big baby. He made Catherine dress up as a soldier and kept his hunting dogs next to the bed. The smell made Catherine gag. Even so, the dogs were probably a more attractive prospect than her husband, pizza-features. Peter failed to get Catherine up the duff, so there then followed a series of lovers in an attempt to get an heir. No-one seemed to mind that Catherine's children were not Peter's. Peter, meanwhile, was taking a series of very ugly women as lovers. Everyone assumed this was to make Catherine jealous, but old Peter was probably trying to feel a little more comfortable about his own looks.

At the time Russia was fighting Prussia to try and take the P off the front of its name. Peter secretly admired the Prussians and dressed in their uniforms. When Empress Elizabeth died, Peter was made big cheese. This additional power did not improve his personality and Catherine decided on a *coup d'état*. Makes a change from a morale-boosting trip to the hairdressers I suppose. Catherine rode to some army barracks dressed as a soldier and proclaimed herself Empress. This was an anxious time because seizing power depended on the troops supporting her. It might be a bit difficult these days to do what Catherine did, as most soldiers are too busy forming double acts á la Robson and Jerome. Thankfully the soldiers supported Catherine and Peter was forced to abdicate. Whilst in prison, he was killed by a guard during a quarrel, although some suspected Catherine had him killed. Fair enough, he'd only have ruined the view at court.

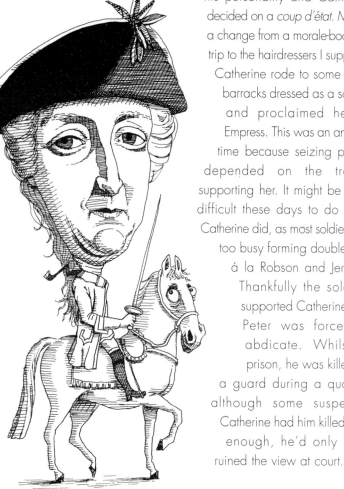

# 'It might be a bit difficult these days to do what Catherine did, as most soldiers are too busy forming double acts á la Robson and Jerome'

Catherine had many lovers but her favourite was Potemkin. He was slovenly, one - eyed and uncouth. He wore caftans and had long unpowdered hair. Perhaps Princess Diana should take a leaf out of Catherine's book and hitch up with Demis Roussos. I bet he can knock up a decent kebab. Although Catherine has a reputation as a beneficent queen, it was not all laughs for the peasants during her reign. Peasant revolts were very harshly put down and in some villages, one in three men were hanged. When things started to go wrong with Potemkin, as inevitably they will with a man in a dress who has the same name as a battleship, Catherine took on a series of ever-younger lovers. She became a bit of a laughing-stock throughout Europe. But I hope she didn't care if she was getting a good seeing-to.

Rumour has it that Catherine went so far as to have sex with a horse and died after rather a heavy one was lowered onto her. (As if anyone could be bothered to set that up without the horse taking them out to dinner first.) This is not true. Catherine died after she had a stroke and fell off a commode. The rumour was probably started by some disgruntled horse whom she'd offended at a party.

Catherine's achievements were great. She presided over a big empire, was a patron of the arts and corresponded with some of the great intellects of the time. Might have been nice though if she'd done a bit more for Russian women instead of just being shafted by young blokes.

# 3 boadicea

There is very little known about Boadicea. In fact, people can't even agree on her name. It could be Boudicca. It could be Boadicca. It could be Bodie - but then she would be a detective in a seventies television series.

*Boadicea takes time off to appear in* **Mother Goose** *in* **Scarborough**

Much of what we know about Boadicea comes from the writings of Roman historians. Unfortunately, in England at that time nobody was interested in writing anything down because they were too busy trying to fight off invaders. Added to this, there was the slight problem that most people couldn't read or write.

However, we do know that Boadicea was royal by birth. This wasn't a great help, though, as all the perks the royal family have these days weren't invented. It just meant you had an extra lick of paint on your chariot. Boadicea was married to King Prasutagus and was part of the Iceni tribe, whose territories lay in Norfolk and Suffolk. This was the best place to have a tribe because Norfolk and Suffolk are very flat and therefore quite easy to drive your chariot over.

The Iceni were a Celtic tribe and they tended to be strong and big-boned with reddish-blond hair. They loved personal adornments and parties. Hey – they were Fergie and Chris Evans. The Iceni had been subdued by the Romans who were on their way round Europe at the time doing a bit of civilising. This meant killing lots of people and making the rest slaves. I wouldn't call that civilised. They should have invited them to dinner and told them which knife to use.

> ## 'The Iceni were a Celtic tribe and they tended to be strong and big-boned with reddish-blond hair. They loved personal adornments and parties. Hey – they were Fergie and Chris Evans'

When Prasutagus died (probably from the exhaustion of trying to get people to pronounce his name properly) he left some money to the Romans and some in trust for his daughters. The Romans weren't having this though – they wanted the whole lot. They took the money, and, just to show there were no hard feelings, had Boadicea flogged and her daughters raped.

This was deliberate Roman policy to show the natives who was boss and to make sure that they never took up arms against them. Wrong – the Iceni took up arms. The Romans weren't too worried about this, however, especially when they realised that Boadicea was going to lead the troops. The Romans believed women were incapable of rule because they were unable to be disciplined. Wrong again Romans.

Cato had written: 'Woman is a violent and uncontrolled animal...' With this attitude to women it's possible he may not have had a girlfriend and was dating a badger which was a bit of a handful.

On the eve of the battle (after having laid out her socks and pants very neatly to prove she was disciplined) Boadicea released a hare from the folds of her dress which was seen by her people as a favourable divination. Lots of you are probably thinking, what a bunch of idiots! But I bet loads of you read your stars in *Cosmo*. Boadicea prayed to the war goddess, Andraste, who must have been in a good mood that night because the Iceni did rather well. They swept down upon Camulodunum (Colchester) with 120,000 troops. The Romans were confident that they could easily resist these painted gingers. Wrong. The Iceni had a fifth column in the town and there were no walls, so invading was a piece of piss. Sometimes you're just so busy raping and the like, that getting a few bricks laid is way down your list of priorities.

*Bet this statue was a bugger to pose for. Rumour has it the horses were so knackered afterwards, they ended up as Pedigree Chum*

Boadicea had the Romans on the run for a bit, so much so, that they abandoned London as she advanced. Supposedly, Boadicea had a chariot with big knives on the wheels which cut peoples' legs off as it passed. This is probably not true, though I wouldn't mind a shopping trolley á la Boadicea on a Friday night in Sainsburys when the housewife stampede gets going.

## 'Sometimes you're just so busy raping and the like, that getting a few bricks laid is way down your list of priorities'

The Iceni launched a ferocious attack on London and were responsible for some inhuman cruelty. I won't go into details about it because if you're into that sort of thing, I'd rather you weren't reading this book. Once London was sorted, the gang headed for St Albans. A final battle with the Romans took place, but, unfortunately, no one knows where that was. Perhaps we should all write to Tony Robinson on *Timewatch* and ask him if he can find it.

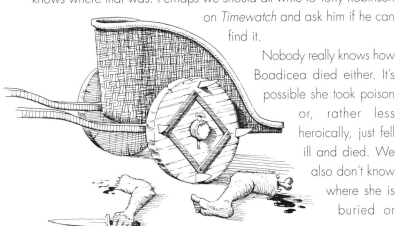

Nobody really knows how Boadicea died either. It's possible she took poison or, rather less heroically, just fell ill and died. We also don't know where she is buried or what her daughters were called. It's possible she is buried at Stonehenge and that her daughters are called Beatrice and Eugenie, but I doubt it.

The Romans exacted a savage revenge, but it was a nail in the coffin of their occupation. They eventually pulled out leaving us to the Dark Ages during which time nobody had a wash or knew which fork to use.

Engrav'd for
COWLEY'S
History of England.

BOADICEA, QUEEN of the ICENI.
animating the Britons to recover their Liberty.

# florence nightingale <sub>came</sub>

from a very rich family who had lots of houses. In those days women of upper class families weren't exactly taxed intellectually. It was assumed she'd go to a few dances and then get married to a posh bloke. Florence obviously wasn't happy with the sort of simpering empty life people like Fergie and Diana led before they tied the knot. She wanted to do something that didn't involve twelve ski-ing holidays a year or shopping at Harvey Nichols for something she'd wear once and then use as a duster.

*Florence often liked to pose for portraits with her pet potato 'Spud'*

Florence had a visionary plan of setting up a hospital. Her parents were alarmed. This may have been because rich people never lifted a finger except when they had a cup of tea and stuck it out to show they were upper class. Or it may have been because the image of nurses at that time was less than flattering. 'Nurses' at that time meant coarse old brutal women swigging on the gin. A mixture of Hattie Jacques and Barbara Windsor in *Carry On. . .* then. Nurses were also immoral and sobriety amongst them was almost unknown. (A couple of elements that attracted me to the job.)

Florence was so obsessed with becoming a nurse that on family holidays she used to nip off and visit the local hospitals. I have to say that even though I enjoyed my nursing job I drew the line at visiting hospitals when I was on holiday – voluntarily, anyway. Florence became very depressed because she could not do what she wanted to do. At the age of thirty-one, she wrote, 'I see nothing desirable except death'. This sounds very serious indeed, but when I looked back through my old teenage diaries, I had written the same thing every other day. Maybe she was a bit pissed or had got on the scales and discovered she'd put on two pounds after eating nothing but carrots for three weeks.

## 'Florence became superintendent of a charitable nursing home in Harley Street. (Not exactly hands on in the slums is it?)'

However, it worked as far as her family were concerned because eventually they let her have her own way. Florence became superintendent of a charitable nursing home in Harley Street. (Not exactly hands on in the slums is it?) Still, the hard work was about to begin. When she was aged thirty-four, the Crimean War broke out and Florence left for Constantinople. In those days, this was quite something for a rich girl to do. I know Fergie hosts the odd charity dinner, but you can't really see her out in Bosnia running a field hospital can you?

Florence went to Scutari, which was a suburb of Constantinople. Wounded men were shipped from the Crimea to Scutari, which was hundreds of miles away and could take two weeks to get to. They probably didn't have a hospital nearer due to the Crimean health cuts. When Florence arrived in Scutari, she found a completely rotten hospital with a cesspool underneath it. What a joy that must have been for all the war-weary soldier boys expecting tender care and finding they were lying above a jobby jacuzzi. Florence decided she was going to sort this whole mess out and laid into it like a kind of Supersloane. The soldiers must have been saying to themselves, 'Is it a bird? Is it a plane? Yes, it's a posh bird!'

Supersloane's work was strapped by bureaucracy. Nothing's changed in the health service then. There are so many managers in the health service now that eventually no-one will get any treatment, but at least the information will all be very nicely photocopied in triplicate and logged onto a computer somewhere.

*The wonderful thing about nurses is that, no matter how depressed or terminally ill you are, their smiling countenance and breezy demeanour make you want to believe in life*

In Scutari, Florence discovered all the bed linen was washed in cold water. Yum, bet that was lovely to slip into. Florence set up a boiler room. Well, got someone to do it for her. She wasn't that hands-on. Florence had somewhat of a dramatic effect on the patients too. Before she arrived all the men swore like troopers, because that's what they were probably. As soon as Florence started tiptoeing down the corridors a miraculous transformation occurred. The swearing stopped and the hospital became as 'holy as a church'. I can't believe this was all achieved solely by Florence's goodness without the help of a little laudanum or bromide in the tea. Surely she must have bashed a couple of them round the head with her lamp.

# 'Fortunately, Florence had brought her own food. (I'm warming to the woman.)'

It does have to be said that women do have somewhat of a civilising influence on men. Not quite enough in my opinion. Now if Florence had gone out to the Crimea and stopped them all killing each other I would have been really impressed. Still, old Flo did have

a massive effect on the health of the soldiers in her care. The death rate dropped dramatically after she got there and she set up a reading room and gave lectures and classes. The officers said she was 'spoiling the brutes'. They were probably peeved that the plebs had decent conditions, as officers all tended to come from the upper echelons of society and spent a lot of the war swanning about with a glass of brandy saying things like 'Top hole Binky!' The soldiers also began to drink less and save their

*Florence's early attempts at bandaging heads prompted her careers master to suggest a career in anything except nursing*

pay. This is getting a bit ridiculous now isn't it? From cursing, hard-drinking monsters to thrifty, well-behaved little angels. Tedious or wot?

Once Florence had emasculated the soldiers at Scutari, she went off to inspect hospitals in the Crimea. Army bigwigs were not amused and a certain Sir John Hall made sure no food went with her to try and stop her poking her nose in. Fortunately, Florence had brought her own food. (I'm warming to the woman.) The legend could have stopped here, but it didn't. Florence lived for more than fifty years after the Crimea. She tried to reform the military hospital system and was responsible for a royal commission on the health of the army. She also got involved in setting up the Nightingale Training School for Nurses. It was said of the nursing school that it had taught 'ladies to be nurses and nurses to be ladies'. Yuk. I've gone right off her again.

# unity mitford

Picture the scene . . . our heroine sits at the feet of the one she loves while he strokes her hair. Aah, how sweet. Unfortunately, the loved one is Hitler and our heroine is Unity Mitford, upper class fascist. She had swastikas in her bedroom, she would pray in front of Hitler's photograph and Hitler saw her as the epitome of Aryan womanhood. So where did it all go wrong for Unity?

## 'Strangely enough, at this point, people began to avoid her. This was probably to do with the fact that she wore a swastika, signed herself with one and talked continuously about Hitler'

As always, a lot can be laid at the feet of her family. They were nostalgic and backward-looking, the sort of people who say, 'It was better in the old days' when 'the old days' were the height of the Spanish Inquisition. Unity's grandfather was a friend of Wagner, himself a right - wing anti-semitic loser, and Unity's middle name was Valkyrie; a bit of a bugger at school registration that one I bet.

Unity was a big, ungainly girl with fair hair and she was pretty odd. She would sit and stare her father out, until he started shouting at her. She would probably have done this to her mother as well, but her mother did a lot of embroidery so she wasn't looking up very often.

# a load of old ball crunchers

Unity's mother also did 'good works', although what that might mean for a woman from that family I can't imagine. Perhaps she killed rabbits before she skinned them. Unity was very close to her sister, Diana, who was very deeply influenced by Oswald Moseley, leader of the British fascist movement. Dear, oh dear, what a family! To have one fascist daughter may be regarded as a misfortune, to have two looks like carelessness.

*Unity caught red-handed with Bob Monkhouse's missing joke books, which explains the expression on her face*

Moseley's fascist movement became a bit more fashion-conscious after he went to visit Mussolini and saw all the Italian fascists wearing black shirts. Either that, or they were all a touch overweight and wanted to look a bit slimmer. Unity was very close to Oswald Moseley, too and he gave Unity the emblem from his lapel. Wearing it, she went to the fascist party headquarters to try and join. They all thought she was a posh twat and far too frivolous to join a serious adult party. (Wrong, boys.) She tried again in Oxford where she told the men there that she knew Moseley and this time she was handed a membership card.

Strangely enough, at this point, people began to avoid her. This was probably to do with the fact that she wore a swastika, signed herself with one and talked continuously about Hitler. It must have been his stunning good looks that first got her hooked. Unity also became fanatically anti-semitic. On a trip to Selfridges, a friend suggested they went into a booth and recorded their voices for a laugh. Now most of us would have attempted a rather crappy rendering of 'I Will Survive', but the friend was alarmed to hear Unity repeating over and over again 'The yids, the yids, we've got to get rid of the yids.' Someone should have got rid of her at that point I think.

# 'She was introduced to Hitler and remarked that there was no-one else in the world she wanted to meet. Must have been his soft, gentle voice'

Unity went to art school in 1933, just long enough to call herself an art student. I would imagine, given the political climate of most art schools, it was just long enough not to get her head kicked in as well. In 1933, Hitler held his first Nuremburg rally (not a driving event), not to be confused with the later Nuremberg Trials (not a riding event). Unity was chosen to go as a member of the British Union of Fascists. She LOVED it. She was introduced to Hitler and remarked that there was no-one else in the world she wanted to meet. Must have been his soft, gentle voice. Unity was so taken with Hitler and the gang that, in 1934, she told her parents she wanted to go and live in Germany. Her parents started to get a little teensy bit worried about her at this point. They were no more than weedy armchair fascists like Garry Bushell on valium and any kind of action scared them, (like lots of racists in this country). So, as a compromise, and to prevent Unity goose-stepping off into the sunset, they sent her to a finishing school in Munich. The school wasn't much better in terms of morals and the girls were taught to avert their eyes if a Jew was being beaten up. Unity, ever moderate in her opinions, was supposed to have remarked, 'Jolly good, serves them right, we should go and cheer'. The head of the school became alarmed at this point. You see, she didn't mind her girls ignoring people getting a good beating, but she certainly didn't want them to enjoy it. I can't see the difference myself.

# a load of old ball crunchers

The headmistress was even more pissed off when Unity brought SS men back to the house, but like the old ostrich she was, I'm sure she managed to ignore it. Unity was determined to meet Hitler. Must have been his humanism and love for his fellow beings. She found out where he went to eat and sat there until she was invited to join him. Must have been that gorgeous moustache.

It is not thought likely Unity and Adolf ever indulged in a leg-over situation although all of Hitler's retinue thought she was in love with him. Hitler seemed to like her because she was posh. Typical snobbery you get from know-nothing scumbags, I suppose. It began to dawn on people that not only was Unity a personality-disordered moron, but she was a grass as well. It was not safe to criticise Nazis in her presence, unless you actually did want to be arrested within the next forty-eight hours. Diana eventually married Moseley and the couple and Unity were invited to the 1936 Olympic games. Hitler sat Unity and his girlfriend, Eva Braun, together. The pair hated each other, although I fail to see how any woman could fight another for the affections of the Führer. Must have been his beautiful haircut.

Wild stories circulated which included a rumour that Hitler had asked Unity to marry him, but it seemed the pair were growing apart. By 1938, access to Hitler was not so easy for Unity. However, she was given a flat by him. How kind, you might think, until you discover it was a flat that a family of Jews had been thrown out of. At this point Unity was becoming very deranged. She told a friend that when she had to quit Germany she would kill herself. When war was declared, she went to the Ministry of the Interior and handed in her badges, wrote a farewell letter to Hitler, went to the English Garden and shot herself in the head. So, at least she was true to her word. However, she was a crap shot and did not die. Doctors left the bullet where it was as it was too dangerous to operate. Hitler visited her in hospital. Is there no end to this man's kindness?

# 'It is not thought likely Unity and Adolf ever indulged in a leg-over situation'

Unity returned to England and went to church regularly. This seems mighty hypocritical to me. Eventually she was taken by her mum to live on the coast of Mull. In 1948, the bullet started to cause trouble and she died of meningitis. I cling to the belief that a world run by women would be a better place than the world as it is today. Unity Mitford and those like her rather put the kibosh on that theory I'm afraid.

# 6 moll cutpurse

was famous in London in the seventeenth century and it's not exactly difficult to work out what she did for a living, is it children?

Moll, whose real name was Mary Frith, was huge, dressed like a man and smoked like a chimney, so she was very unlikely to come anywhere in a Miss World contest. Good. The daughter of a shoemaker, she was a very difficult child and hated sewing. Considering that I find sewing nearly as exciting as ingrowing toenails, I can sympathise with her view. Moll also found girls boring and would tear off her cap and go and fight boys on the street. This was also one of my hobbies when I was young. Moll grew into a plain woman. (Yes, some of us know how it feels, old girl.) Her parents sent her into service but she was hopeless at it. She hated kids and frequently lost her temper with them and went out and got pissed. I used to work for Dr Barnardos and I wasn't too

*At that time Peckham consisted of a church and two houses, but the industry for which it is now world-famous was already well established*

keen on kids either, but I used to lose my temper when they went out and got pissed.

Moll's relatives were ashamed of her. Normally if you are ashamed of your relatives, you pretend you don't know them or at the very most send them a parcel of dog poo. Moll's relatives were a bit more serious about it. They tried to trick her into getting on to a ship in the harbour bound for the New World. When Moll realised what was going on, she jumped off and swam back to the shore. Not a particularly bright family, by the sound of it. All Moll had to do was ask where the ship was going and hey presto! dastardly plot has failed. After the very clever trick incident, Moll decided never to go near her relatives again. Fair enough. They might have tried to poison her with a cup of poison with 'poison' written on it.

Moll went off with a group of fortune tellers, but soon got bored with them because the *'If anyone comes anywhere near me, I'll shove this right up their Gary Glitter'*
money wasn't good enough. So she decided on a life of crime and joined a gang of pickpockets instead. It was at this point that Moll began wearing men's clothes. She had assessed her situation, realised she had no charm or looks and therefore very little hope of a husband. In those days having a husband was much more important than it is today, although sad phrases like 'on the shelf' still

exist as though some women were unattractive products that have not been purchased. If that is the case, I am the last Ronco Buttoneer left on the shelf in Woolies.

Rumour abounded that Moll was a hermaphrodite. This was not true. Human beings have always had a facility for gossip-mongering about people who are a bit out of the ordinary. They seem not to like anyone different, far less anyone different who seems to be perfectly happy with their life. There are rumours floating around that I am a lesbian, which I assume were started by men who were really jealous that I was such a looker yet so unattainable.

**'Sad phrases like on the shelf still exist as though some women were unattractive products that have not been purchased. If that is the case, I am the last Ronco Buttoneer left on the shelf in Woolies'**

It was at this point Moll became Ms Cutpurse, because people in the seventeenth century wore purses like bumbags and Moll was extremely skilful at c——g them off. (Fill in the missing word, so I can check you're concentrating.) Moll was not that brillliant at the job though, because she did get caught and sent to prison several times. This put her off the pickpocketing game and she decided to become a highwaywoman. (Obviously these days, they are called highwaypersons). Moll became a friend of the famous highwayman

Captain Hind, so famous I've never heard of him. Moll was a royalist, so she only robbed Roundheads, which was a bit stupid because they didn't have nearly as much dosh. In one incident, she robbed an army captain and shot him. He was determined to get her and did and she was sent to Newgate prison. She bribed her way out of Newgate for £2000 and bought a house in Fleet Street. People in the area were still not keen on her wearing men's gear and she was called to court to answer the offence of wearing 'indecent and manly apparel'. Maybe we could bring that sort of law back

> **'Moll was a royalist, so she only robbed Roundheads, which was a bit stupid because they didn't have nearly as much dosh'**

and call people to court for wearing indecent and hideous shell-suits.

Moll's punishment for her clothes was to do penance at St Paul's Cross wearing a white sheet. What I wear, in fact, when I'm going to a fancy dress party as Alaska. Moll turned up for her penance and wept as though she really regretted it. Everyone was very impressed until they realised she was pissed out of her bonce, having poured six pints of wine down her neck. We all know what it's like to get maudlin on the booze. Last time I got really drunk I started weeping because I haven't got a husband and when I sobered up . . . I carried on because it was such a pathetic thing to cry about.

Despite this incident Moll didn't hang up her Y-fronts and slip into a little chiffon number, she bet someone she could ride from Charing Cross to Shoreditch in men's clothes (quite a long way). Crowds along the route were not impressed and threatened to pull her off her horse, but she did it all the same.

After that it seemed to be time for Moll to calm down a bit. She became a fence, receiving stolen goods, and lived comfortably in a big house with some dogs and parrots. She was reported to be 'mightily taken with the pastime of smoking'. Of course in those days, smoking was a pastime as opposed to the leprous, sinful, repulsive, anti-social crime it is these days. In later years, Moll converted her house into a brothel and became part of a world which included prostitutes and transvestites with names like Aniseed Water Robin who wore skirts and petticoats. This of course is not such a big shock as half the members of the judiciary do this in their spare time.

## 'Despite this incident Moll didn't hang up her Y-fronts and slip into a little chiffon number'

Despite her fondness for smoking and the cornucopia of hideous diseases that were around, Moll managed to survive to the age of seventy-three. She left instructions that she was to be buried face down to be as preposterous in death as in life. Also anyone who dug her up would get a great view, I suppose.

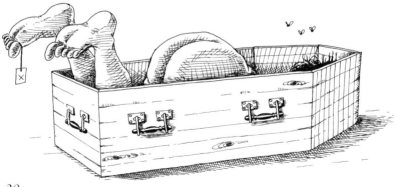

# marie antoinette

was born in 1755 and was destined to marry into the French royal family. She was the daughter of Marie Therese of Austria and as a child played with the prodigy Mozart. Unfortunately most child prodigies are horrendous little monsters, so she probably got pinched a lot. She would have been better off sticking with Mozart though, compared to what she had coming in the form of her future husband.

## 'The Dauphin Louis was so short-sighted he couldn't recognise friends at three paces. Always a good excuse for not getting a round in'

The Dauphin Louis was the grandson of Louis XV and was so short-sighted he couldn't recognise friends at three paces. Always a good excuse for not getting a round in, though. He was also not very bright and about the only thing he liked doing was hunting. Still, Marie Antoinette didn't have any say in the matter so they were married. On their wedding night Louis wrote 'rien' or 'nothing' in his diary because he couldn't get it up. Apparently all he needed was a fairly simple operation to sort out his impotence, but he was too scared, so he didn't have it for seven years. Poor old Marie Antoinette, I expect even Louis looked stunningly attractive after about four years.

# a load of old ball crunchers

Marie Antoinette recorded her average day in her diary and for those of you who think it might have been pretty exciting to be queen of France . . . get a load of this.

Up at ten, prayers, breakfast, see aunts, hair done, see visitors, dress, mass, lunch, see husband, read/write, aunts, singing, aunts, supper, bed.

Rather too large a sprinkling of aunts for me there. Still, just the one dose of husband makes up for it, I suppose. Maybe Louis popped in to see Marie Antoinette and because of his poor vision, ended up talking to the Yucca for an hour.

*For the richest woman in the world, she doesn't half look peaky. Perhaps what she really said was, 'Let them eat cake, I'm sticking to Complan.' Deserved to die*

You might think with all the power Marie Antoinette had, she was tempted to dabble in politics. Considering the poor girl couldn't even spell one of her own middle names when she was fifteen, it didn't look likely. Also, her mother didn't want her involved in politics. 'She doesn't know a thing. . .', she said supportively of Marie Antoinette, so her daughter concentrated hard on being a fluffy bunny and filling her head with nothing.

In 1774 Louis XV got smallpox and died, as you tended to in those days if you got anything worse than a slight sniffle, so the Dauphin and Dauphine were pronounced King and Queen. The royal couple lived at the Palace of Versailles and the excess that was displayed there was one of the reasons the French people eventually had enough and did that funky revolution thang. I've been to Versailles . . . the caff there was crap. Not quite as crap as the results of some of the ridiculous etiquette practised at the palace. For example, if the First Lady of Honour or First Waiting Woman were absent, Marie Antoinette couldn't have a drink of water, as only they were allowed to serve her. Of course she couldn't get her fat arse off the chair and get it herself, because she was the Queen. It took seven people to dress her in the morning, the hopeless old trout, although one of her fashion habits did survive well into 80s soap operas like *Dallas* and *Dynasty*: Marie Antoinette was the original proponent of big hair. She had her hair combed upwards to a height of eighteen inches, so maybe she did look quite like a Yucca plant. On top of the hair went three-foot-long plumes and the hair itself would be decorated with miniature scenes like a garden. No wonder Louis may have got confused. The whole hairstyle was topped off with loads of jewels, creating what sounds like a hairy sparkly Kew Gardens. Still, it probably fended off the aunts for a couple of hours.

## 'It took seven people to dress her in the morning, the hopeless old trout'

Silly Louis XVI had no control over his silly wife. She actually built a village at Petit Trianon near Versailles so that she and her rich friends could play at being peasants. They milked cows and dressed up as shepherdesses for a laugh. Good job the Press wasn't too hot in those days or the French Revolution might have happened a lot sooner than it did. Louis, having eventually had all his creative equipment jiggled about, finally managed to get Marie Antoinette pregnant and she had a daughter called Marie Therese Charlotte. The birth sounds a

# a load of old ball crunchers

bit of a nightmare given that it was the right of fifty peers to be present. Fifty peers a-peering must have driven her mad; still you know blokes, most of them probably fainted at the first sign of yukkiness. Marie Antoinette also had a son and although she didn't realise it she was starting to get very unpopular with the masses.

People began to call her 'the Austrian bitch'. At the age of thirty-two Marie Antoinette started to calm down a bit, but it was too late, the damage was done. She also seemed to be genuinely fond of her husband, which was a good job as he was about the only person in France who liked her, or maybe he couldn't see her properly and just smiled to be polite when she came into the room.

The French Revolution was not really about starving peasants, but had more to do with poverty in towns. It started when the Third Estate of the commons split from the clergy and the nobles at a meeting at Versailles, calling itself the National Assembly. Its members were locked out of the meeting hall and that is when the trouble began. Barricades were set up in Paris and the Bastille was stormed, which was a bit of a let-down as there were only seven prisoners in there. A bit like breaking into an animal laboratory and finding just the one beagle working his way through twenty Benson and Hedges.

After the initial violence some posh people started to leg it out of the country, but nevertheless, despite the atmosphere, a great banquet was held at Versailles which really pissed everyone off (except those who were invited, of course). A women's march through the streets was organised with a lot of men disguised as women. (Bound to get nasty then.) The march headed for Versailles and demonstrated under Marie Antoinette's window. She rang to find out what was going on. I know she could have just looked out of the window, but the First Looking Out Of The Window Lady wasn't there. Some demonstrators broke through, shouting 'We are going to cut off her head, tear out her heart, fry her liver and eat it and that won't be the end of it'. Whether they had any vegetarian recipes, I don't know. The mob burst into Marie Antoinette's bedroom but she managed to leave just in time by a secret door. Two bodyguards were caught and beheaded but then Marie Antoinette came out on the balcony and the atmosphere changed completely. The crowd started to shout, 'Vive la reine, vive la bodyguard'. (I'm sure the two poor buggers who'd already copped it weren't too impressed.)

The royal family were taken to the capital twelve miles away, which took six hours, roughly the time it takes today on the French equivalent of the North Circular. There they planned an escape from imprisonment. They got false passports, but, unfortunately, Marie Antoinette cocked it all up by insisting she took nearly her whole wardrobe, so that they had to use a huge bright yellow coach to accommodate all her gear. Because they had to travel so slowly they were caught before they reached safety.

Back in Paris, Louis was sentenced to death. Eventually, Marie Antoinette went on trial, too, and was sentenced to the guillotine. We don't even know if she managed to pick up a few knitting tips whilst trundling past all the old ladies purling and plaining *en route* to the scaffold. On her way up the steps, Marie Antoinette trod on someone's foot. Her last words were an apology. Historically memorable? No. Polite, though.

# 8

# mary queen of scots' parents

were James V of Scotland and Mary of Guise. Her mother had already had two sons who died in infancy. That's what you called two really bad heir days. Mary of Guise also had bad hair days too, as she thought that greasy hair caused colds. She therefore advised everyone, including her daughter Mary, to wash their hair at least once a month. Vidal Sassoon would have a blue fit.

James was not impressed with the birth of Mary, so unimpressed in fact that he died five days later. Mary was crowned at the age of nine months in Stirling Castle, but wasn't a very good queen at this point because she couldn't do much except gurgle. At the age of six, she went to France (with a bit of help) and lived there until she was sixteen. As an adolescent, she had gastric troubles which she was to suffer from for the rest of her life, Rennie Rapeze not being available in those days.

## 'A worse omen might have been if Mary had taken her head off for a bit'

When Mary was fifteen an arranged marriage took place between her and Francis of France. The whole ceremony in Notre Dame cathedral took hours and Mary had to take the crown off because it was too heavy for her. Many people thought this was a bad omen. A worse omen might have been if Mary had taken her head off for a bit. Francis's dad, the king, liked a bit of a joust and one day, despite warnings from his wife, decided to have one last joust before he went home. This turned out to be a mistake. He got a splinter in his eye and one in his throat. These went septic and he had jousted his last. Mary became Queen of France at the age of sixteen.

The French court didn't stay in one place for very long due to paranoia about plots and also the obligation to visit people. Any plotting was dealt with in a very harsh way as one plotter discovered when he was hanged in front of the court just after they'd had their dinner. I bet lots of the diners didn't get round to their After Eights.

Mary's mother, who was still back in Scotland acting as Queen Regent, got dropsy and dropped dead. Mary was not told about her death for ten days as everyone was worried about her reaction. Added to this, Francis, her husband, was not a healthy boy. He had

foetid breath and red blotches all over his face; a prime candidate for the bag-over-the-head treatment. People said he needed to bathe in the blood of young children to stay healthy and peasants would hide their kids when he passed, possibly as much to do with the halitosis as the children's blood story. Francis's health continued to get worse. His ear was squirting pus, for which he was given a massive dose of rhubarb. Don't laugh; it cured him for a bit. All right, do laugh; he died a few weeks later, aged sixteen.

*In the olden days, sometimes the only bit of entertainment to be had was to be shown a piece of cloth for several hours*

# a load of old ball crunchers

Despite his shortcomings, Mary was heartbroken, although it was not long before the question of another husband reared its ugly head. And talking of ugly heads, one of the candidates was Don Carlos, the Spanish heir. He was five and a half stone, and had one shoulder higher than the other – quite a dish in Elizabethan times. He had also fallen down the stairs and after a spot of head-drilling (or trepanning if you're intelligent) he started to have homicidal fits. Thankfully this unmissable opportunity passed Mary by. Her cousin Lord Darnley had come to express his condolences, and by Elizabethan standards Darnley was a sex-god, as he was good looking, his shoulders matched and he wasn't covered in pock-marks.

> ## 'By Elizabethan standards Darnley was a sex-god, as he was good looking, his shoulders matched and he wasn't covered in pock-marks'

Now that Mary's French husband had snuffed it, Mary had to return to Scotland. Her cousin Elizabeth I refused her safe passage, but Mary went anyway. The highlands of Scotland in those days were a bit like the Wild West and many people still believed in witchcraft. John Knox, the Ian Paisley of his day, had just produced his 'First Blast of the Trumpet Against the Monstrous Regiment of Women' whom he thought were 'weak, foolish, frail, impatient and feeble'. I'd have punched him into shape.

Mary's grand plan was a reconciliation with Elizabeth and conciliation with her subjects. Sad how things just never work out the way you want them to. Mary fell madly in love with Darnley, so much

*Mary never truly understood the English. Particularly the penchant of Newcastle fans for painting their hats and mandolins in team colours*

so that they married before a special dispensation arrived. (Maybe this is the origin of the old faithful heckle put-down, 'Isn't it a shame when cousins marry'.) As with most psychotic love affairs where you eat, drink and sleep the person, it all went horribly wrong fairly quickly. Darnley was sulky that his name kept appearing after Mary's on official bits of paper and he really wanted to be King, instead of just Mary's tart. He was a natural born plotter. Mary had a secretary called Riccio of whom she was very fond. Darnley, with some other plotters, murdered Riccio at a supper party Mary was having. I hope Ariel Colour managed to sort out the stains on the tablecloth. The plot fell apart though and Darnley was won back by Mary although he sulked massively about it. The other plotters disbanded and left Scotland.

Mary was pregnant, and when she went into labour, she attempted by means of witchcraft to give her pains to someone else; always a bit risky compared to an epidural, and it didn't work, surprisingly enough. However Mary got through labour and had a son, James. Darnley didn't last much longer. People in those days who pissed the royals off normally ended up six feet under. A series of letters, known as 'the casket letters', which Mary had written to James Earl of Bothwell, came into play and implicated Mary in the murder of her husband. These days, if you bump off your old man you wouldn't get away with it, even if you are a royal. You can of course try to bump off your boyfriend by sucking all the blood out of him

# a load of old ball crunchers

through his toe, but it takes forever.

Needless to say the casket letters disappeared in the way that evidence does. Mary didn't waste any time though. The Earl of Bothwell had captured her but after some token resistance she married him. One would have thought Barbara Cartland might have written the plot for this. However in Barbara's books there is a happy ending. . . not so for poor old Mary.

When the Scottish Lords rose against her, she fled to England, only to be put in prison. Out of the frying pan into Elizabeth's wok. There were several Catholic plots to get Mary on the throne of England, none of which worked. Mary lived in semi-confinement until the Babington plot (yet another attempt to get her on the throne) was foiled. At this point Elizabeth had had enough. Mary was brought to trial. Perhaps the Babington plotters, being good Catholics, kept saying 'Guilty' all the time. Mary was executed in 1587 at the age of forty-five. I suppose the one good thing for her was that she didn't have to go through the menopause. Not much of a consolation if you don't have a head, though.

# janis joplin

was the ultimate wild, hippy chick. In the sixties and seventies, female hippies were called chicks. Male hippies weren't called cocks, I don't know why.

Janis was born in Port Arthur, Texas and as a child was a voluminous reader and thumb-sucker. The thumb-sucking drove her parents mad and when she was nine they tried to stop her by preventing her listening to

*anis always
*xaggerated about the
*enis size of her latest
*eau*

her favourite radio show. Janis had the most massive tantrum they had ever seen. Her oral and aural fixations were vying for position. My parents tried to stop me sucking my thumb by putting mustard on it when I was a kid. No wonder I'm a hot dog fan.

As a teenager, Janis put on loads of weight and her skin became very bad. These are almost the two worst things that can happen to you when you are a teenager, apart from not being allowed to read Smash Hits. Because of the grief Janis got from other kids, she became outrageous, swore a lot and shocked even the boys. To be honest it doesn't take much to shock boys, because of their expectations of girls. All you have to do is step on a couple of their conkers. Janis dressed outlandishly, which in those days meant not being within ten feet of any crimplene. She was called 'pig' by the other kids and would laugh, but go home and cry about it later. That's the problem with us women, we're too sensitive. She should have gone home and planned her revenge. Still, as schoolchildren in America appear to be shooting each other at every opportunity, maybe it's as well she didn't.

Janis also boasted about sex, more to wind the locals up than anything else. She was probably still a virgin. No - one wanted to check because they remembered her reaction to the radio/thumb-sucking incident.

Janis was very bright, so understandably her parents were worried when she began to hang around with beatniks. Beatniks were scruffy herberts with beards who didn't wash and had holes in their clothes. Janis liked progressive jazz, but this may have been because she hadn't washed her ears for a bit and couldn't hear it properly, as to most of us it sounds like a hamster being trodden on. Janis had a good voice. One of her teachers remarked that it was a lot more pleasant than 'the caterwauling she did later'.

# 'If a bloke turns you down, the option of turning him into a six-foot pink rabbit before your very eyes is a tempting one'

In 1961 Janis ran off to Houston on a drinking binge. When she came back she saw a psychiatrist. Bit extreme, but that's Americans for you. Janis left home and went to Los Angeles where she stayed with an aunt for a bit. She must have realised that this wouldn't turn her into a hard-rocking, drug-taking out of control pop legend so she moved to Venice, the beatnik area, and started to sing in public. The caterwauling seemed to go down quite well. Her first recording was a jingle for a bank. Mmm. . . very 'flowers in your hair' and 'don't bogart that joint'.

At the University of Texas, Janis formed a band, the Waller Street Boys, and began singing in a variety of different styles. She also experimented with drugs like grass and seconal and began behaving in a variety of styles including drunkenly throwing a woman down the stairs and running into buildings headfirst. No wonder her hair looked such a mess. Eventually Janis was drawn to San Francisco where she found that because of her drug habit she wasn't a misfit any more. However Janis had a bad year in 1963 when she was brutally mauled by some yobboes in a back alley and then had a serious bike accident, possibly due to running at a bike with her head.

Janis had crap relationships with men and was becoming a speed freak and starting to deal drugs herself. I dare say these were related. If a bloke turns you down, the option of turning him into a six-foot pink rabbit before your very eyes is a tempting one. In 1965, Janis tried to commit herself to hospital saying she was crazy. The hospital wouldn't let her in. One would imagine that the hospital was groaning under the weight of a million pungent beatniks and just didn't have room for another

*Janis was a true professional, even practising her mike technique on the toilet*

one. There was no other option now for Janis except to fall in with a charming psychotic methadrine addict, and so she did. This charming man wanted to marry her (Rule Number One: Never trust a proposal from a charming methadrine addict). Janis, sadly, believed him and returned to Port Arthur to prepare for her wedding. The charming man predictably bogged off and left Janis heartbroken. She joined a new band, Big Brother and The Holding Company. I hope they were big brothers to her and they did hold her a bit because by now she was very pissed off.

Janis was a total scruff-bag, which is a state many women are condemned to, including myself. This is because whenever I put anything smart on, for some reason, within seconds, a portion of meat curry will fly through the air onto my chest. Consequently to fit in with an equally sartorially-elegant gang, Janis became pally with some Hell's Angels, who made her look like Bonnie Langford. Janis moved to Haight Ashbury, the famous hippy quarter of San Francisco. She had massive success at the Monterey pop festival and was signed up by Albert Grossman, Bob Dylan's manager. He was an expert in caterwauling, judging by Bob's dulcet tones.

# 'Rule Number One: Never trust a proposal from a charming methadrine addict'

The first gig Janis did in New York had rave reviews. Janis was enchanted by fame, but it didn't change her outlook, which was bleak. She was still wild. She had a fight with Jim Morrison of The Doors. He pulled her hair out and she hit him with a bottle he said belonged to him. Still what's a bit of baldness and a bleeding head between rock stars.

Janis gained loads of weight from heavy drinking and began to display an insatiable appetite for sex. A huge intake of alcohol does allow you to broaden your range of potential bed fellows, because you can't see what they look like for a kick-off. She formed a new band called Kosmic Blues and became obsessed with band member Richard Kermode. Kermode by name, commode by nature I'm afraid, because in her eyes he treated her like shite. The Kosmic Blues album was a mess. Janis was a mess. My bedroom is a mess. Janis was constantly looking for reassurance, asking people if they loved her and being bad-tempered and selfish because of the drugs. Her friends were really worried about her and persuaded her to see a doctor, who told her her liver function was normal. This was a big mistake really for Janis who assumed this meant she could consume several hundred bottles of booze a session without getting ill.

So continued many one night stands, which we are told by psychologists are a rather sad attempt by women to find love. Love? No, I don't think so, but they were sad if you actually had to talk to the bloke in the morning. Janis by now had a serious heroin problem. Help seemed to be at hand in the shape of David Niehaus, her only proper boyfriend. They travelled in South America together and Janis was really happy. However as soon as she came back home she was back on the drugs again and Niehaus left her. Her best friend left too. Janis began calling herself Pearl and picking up pretty boys for sex. She kept saying things like 'nobody loves me'. Funnily enough, no-one pointed out that this would be a good time to see a psychiatrist. She talked of suicide and got heavily into heroin again. In 1970 when Jimmy Hendrix died she said, 'There but for the grace of God go I'.

The last gig she played was to 40,000 people at Harvard stadium. She had met a bloke called Seth Morgan, who was a student (as opposed to an extra from *Emmerdale*. . .

But he couldn't halt the downward trend. Too busy out collecting traffic cones. One Saturday night when she was alone and Seth was going to be a day late, Janis went to bed, overdosed accidentally on heroin and was found dead the next day. A tragic end but probably a more interesting life than Dana.

# rosa luxemburg

was an outsider in many ways. In Poland she was a Jew and in Germany, a foreigner. She was also unusual for a woman at that time because she didn't just want to settle down and be a housewife, she wanted a career as well. This attitude in those days was as rare as a Windsor in the dole office and Rosa suffered as a result.

She was born in 1870, the youngest of five from a comfortable family. (Well off, that is, although they may have been quite nice to sit on too.) As a child, Rosa suffered from a congenital hip dislocation,

*Rosa often went for walks in her nightie when it was hot*

which meant her leg was put in a cast and she had to stay in bed for a year. To me this would be heaven, but I suppose children can't lie there with forty fags and a bottle of stout, so Rosa got very bored. When Rosa was let out of bed, one leg was shorter than the other, and as we all know, humanity tolerates disability about as kindly as Saddam Hussein tolerates discos. Rosa was to battle the limp for the rest of her life.

At the age of twelve, Rosa witnessed a pogrom in which two thousand families suffered losses. She was traumatised by this and it began to shape her views about humanity. (That they were all a bunch of horrible bastards, I would have thought.) At sixteen, Rosa was described as having a severe face and a big chest. At least it wasn't the other way round. Rosa's mother made her dresses which made her frontage look smaller, which probably pissed her off as she might have felt that was all she had going for her. Rosa considered her parents petit bourgeois and started to get in with a load of leftie students. Well, it beats archaeology soc, I suppose. After graduation Rosa joined an underground illegal socialist group. Their aim was to build a workers party. At college I joined the losers group. Their aim was to get through college without joining a group.

## 'At sixteen, Rosa was described as having a severe face and a big chest. At least it wasn't the other way round'

Rosa then met the man who was to make her life a misery. His name was Leo Jogiches and he was a Lithuanian Jew. He had joined the workers movement and was irresistibly drawn to terrorism. People that are irresistibly drawn to things tend to be a bit irresistible themselves, unless of course what they're drawn to is you. Let's face it, not many women like a pushover. Well, not unless it's a very beautiful man whom you can actually push over. By this time Rosa had arrived in Zurich, then a centre for progressive Polish intelligentsia. (Sadly now a centre for snow and boring types who like to go down hills on bits of wood.) Leo Jogisches already had a girlfriend but she was left behind in Zurich when he and Rosa went to Geneva to meet a man called Plekhanov and try and get in with the Russian Marxist Party. Rosa and Jogisches became lovers which must have been quite a shock for Rosa who had never seen Jogisches bare. (Geddit? You will do if you use a Y instead of a J.)

# a load of old ball crunchers

In 1893, Rosa and Leo co-founded the anti-nationalist party, Social Democrats of the Kingdom of Poland. She and Leo (I've done the Yogi Bear joke) rented two rooms in adjacent houses. This was because in those days you had to pretend you weren't nomping. Their party fought with the Polish Socialist Party, as indeed groups who are supposed to have the same views always do. Rosa was made editor in chief of their paper, *The Worker's Cause*. This didn't have horoscopes in it, by the way.

Rosa's cause on the side, Leo, turned out to be 'an angry man' with 'no natural impulse to love'. He expected her to conform to his rules. Irritated by her attempt to change him, Leo wanted to keep their relationship secret. All he was interested in was the revolution. All other entertainments, he thought, were a waste of time. Rosa considered herself his wife, although I might have considered giving him the elbow, as you can't make a leopard change his spots, or indeed a Leo change

**To pull in punters,** The Workers' Cause *fun and games page published a 'Spot the Head of The Socialist International Women's Section'. The rollover prize of five zlotys* **remains unclaimed to this day**

his extremely irritating personality defects. Rosa began to have a great desire to have a child. Leo was not keen, a problem many women have. I don't know the answer, but has anyone ever tried threatening their partner at gunpoint? Rosa was becoming famous and as this happened, so Leo became more critical. He wanted to be the master in private. Big baby.

In 1896, the Polish Social Democratic Party was destroyed and *The Workers Cause* was closed down. Leo became bitter, as if Rosa needed any more crap from him. Rosa herself was doing well, just to wind him up, one assumes. She also married a friend's son, Gustav Lubeck, in order to get German citizenship, and moved to Berlin.

Rosa toured Silesia speaking and what we call in comedy 'doing stormers'. At the same time she was writing articles for journals and participating in the German Social Democratic Party congresses. As far as the party was concerned she was a bit too much of an individual with her own strong views. Most of them would have probably preferred it if she'd made a nice cuppa and some egg sandwiches for the boys. Eventually, after a bit of emotional blackmail Leo agreed to join her after she'd been alone in Berlin for two years. Rosa told her parents Leo was a Swiss citizen (lie) and they were going to get married (lie). She was of course already married, but mum and dad didn't know that. She had to tell a completely different set of lies to the (somewhat moralistic) party and as far as they were concerned Leo was her cousin.

*'hen things began to look bad, Rosa ecided to try her luck on* Stars in heir Eyes *as Martin Luther*

Leo became depressed, and there's nothing worse than a depressed selfish git. He lay on his bed all day whilst Rosa was working her arse off. Rosa tried her best to put a firework up Leo's jacksie but the bugger wouldn't move. Eventually he disappeared off to Algiers with his brother who had TB and Rosa introduced a new strict regime of getting up at the crack of dawn into her life. She began to write a paper aimed at uniting Polish and German workers, which didn't have much of an effect as they just wanted to fight each other. She also had a go at bourgeois women who got involved in politics because they were bored with domesticity. (The ones that aren't bored with domesticity are called Tory ladies.) Rosa was sent to jail in Berlin for insulting Kaiser Wilhelm II in a speech, just because the big-nosed greasy twat didn't like it.

## 'Rosa was becoming famous and as this happened, so Leo became more critical. He wanted to be the master in private. Big baby'

Rosa is perhaps most famous for arguing with Lenin over his interpretations of Marxist theory. She felt he tried to control the party too much instead of letting it grow and develop. She was also opposed to Lenin's idea of armed insurrection. This seems very sensible to me, but the bolshy bolshies didn't like it. They wanted a ruck.

Leo, who'd come back from Algiers, left to work in Krakow. Rosa wrote to him frequently mentioning someone called 'W', probably a Jew from Warsaw called Wladyslaw Feinstein (as opposed to the Kaiser Wilhelm). When Rosa went to see Leo and told him there was another man in her life, he collapsed emotionally. (Bit bloody late.) When Rosa returned to Warsaw she was arrested. She managed to bribe her way out. Poor old Leo got eight years. Meanwhile a bloke called Costia Zetkin had moved into Rosa's flat. He was the son of Clara Zetkin, a well known Marxist activist. When Rosa came back they became lovers. (Well, if it's on a plate. . . or in your house.) Rosa kept their liaison secret and then Leo buggered it all up by escaping from prison, finding out and going berserk. Rosa got a gun because she was scared of him. Eventually, worried about the competition, Costia began to distance himself from her and after a couple of years their relationship ended.

# 'She threw a bar of chocolate at a guard who tried to move a visitor on. . . sacrilege'

In 1913, Rosa delivered a speech urging the German workers not to take up arms against workers of other nationalities. She was threatened with imprisonment and made a superb speech about war in her defence. This really made her a celebrity. (Looking pretty and keeping it shut seems to make you a celebrity today.) Rosa and her attorney Paul Levi became lovers. (Well if it's on a plate. . . or in court with you.) Around about this point the First World War broke out and a small group, including Rosa, got together to form what would become the Spartacus league. (Yep, old Leo was hanging on in there still.) The Spartacists wanted to try and stop the war. They weren't listened to, surprisingly. Rosa herself went to prison and during the war was banged up for three years and four months. At one point she threw a bar of chocolate at a guard who tried to move a visitor on . . . sacrilege.

Rosa wrote a critique of the Russian Revolution based on the fact that Lenin seemed to be eliminating democracy. News came from Russia that Lenin wanted to publish Rosa's collected works but not the critique of the Russian Revolution. (Lenin trying to have his cake and eat it instead of having his chocolate and chucking it.)

After the war Germany was in trouble. Pacifists and Jews were blamed (as usual) for the lack of morale. A republic was proclaimed

# a load of old ball crunchers

and revolution started. The Spartacists produced the Red Flag paper to communicate with the workers. These days of course it would be easier what with telly and radio, except no-one would want to listen because they're all too busy watching Blind Date. Rosa was leading a vagrant life moving from hotel to hotel. The only advantage being that she didn't have to make the bed. She found herself denounced everywhere as a devil, which isn't great for your self esteem. Government troops occupied the offices of the Red Flag, fired on Spartacist demonstrators and left eighteen dead. The chancellor eventually ordered troops to Berlin to fight the Spartacists. A horrible group called the Volunteer Corps battled the Sparticists and mutilated their

bodies. Oh, the joys of civilisation. Rosa was arrested and taken to the Hotel Eden, where she was ordered to prison. On the journey to the prison, she was shot in the head and her body was dumped in the river. At least, these days we can reassure ourselves that this brutal and illegal behaviour wouldn't happen today. Except in Bosnia, Rwanda, Kuwait, Cambodia . . . need I go on.

# george eliot

wasn't really called George – she was called Mary Ann. All will become clear later.

Mary Ann came from a fairly well-off family. She argued with her father a lot about religion and didn't like going to church on Sundays, even though *The Waltons* wasn't on telly then. Mary Ann was an exceptional student and was obsessional about one of her teachers, Maria Lewis, who was a dedicated Evangelist. I'm afraid schoolgirl crushes passed me by. Having spotted twelve yards of dodgy-looking bloomers wrapped round my French teacher's legs, I decided to give it a miss and snog a boy from the local tech instead.

Mary Ann developed an 'insatiable desire for the esteem of her friends'. This can be achieved, I've found, by not blaahing on about religion all the time. But, poor Mary Ann blaahed on about religion all the time. She thought the spirit could only develop if you acknowledged the essential sinfulness and unworthiness of the self. Another

*OK, she's no supermodel, but how many supermodels are great writers? In fact, how many of them can write?*

# a load of old ball crunchers

no-no as far as getting friends is concerned, I think.

When Mary Ann was sixteen, her mother died and she had to run the house. During this time she educated herself and got frustrated because there was no one with whom she could discuss her knowledge. She wrote to friends but they were scared off when she pointed out how sinful they were. These friends would have been the contemporary equivalent of those women who giggle and say, 'My boyfriend knows about politics, ask him'.

Mary Ann had a brother called Isaac, who probably changed his name to Fifi Trixibelle at some point. He married and left Mary Ann alone with her dad. At this point Mary Ann began refusing to go to church. I also indulged in adolescent rebellion, except rather than refusing to go to church, I started getting drunk a lot and dating a local titled man. His title was 'The Man You Would Least Like Your Daughter To Go Out With In Hastings'.

When Mary Ann's dad died, she was taken to Geneva by some friends, the Brays. She didn't want to come home. When I went to Geneva, I couldn't wait to come home. It's too clean and boring - like Jane Seymour. Eventually, however, she went to live in London.

In London, Mary Ann became assistant editor on the *Westminster Review*, a magazine which covered social reform, politics and religion. Although it was not exactly a *True Romance* type of mag, Mary Ann got turned on by it and fell in love with the publisher. However, his wife and mistress were not so keen on her. Three's a bit crowded in a marriage as we know from a certain *Panorama* interview, so four is really pushing it.

Mary Ann was sent to Coventry, literally. But after a while she went back to London and met George Lewes. He was small and ugly and people said he looked like an ape. It was his personality which won people over. As you know, this is not something women can do. A woman's personality is about as valuable as a rack of rings from Ratners. George Lewes was married, too, but he had an open marriage. And, although this was probably for George's benefit, his wife made full use of it – with his best friend. Bit of a pisser, eh?

Mary Ann pointlessly changed her name to Marian at this time, and after George's wife had a second baby by his best friend, she started having a relationship with Lewes. Marian and George left the country and spent eight months in Germany. Marian was convinced of the morality of her decision. Not convinced enough to stay in England and face the music, though.

*George got called a harlot, which in some women's eyes would be an improvement on horseface*

## a load of old ball crunchers

However, they did eventually come back to London and Marian asked people to call her Mrs Lewes. She and George were very happy together. They went on lots of nature holidays where Marian studied sea creatures. She wrote: 'Look at man in the light of a shell fish and he will certainly come off worst in terms of beauty and design of his architecture' (and taste, too).

Women in Marian's time were viewed as intuitive rather than intellectual. At soirées she met many feminists and wrote a piece called 'Silly Novels by Lady Novelists'. For an example of this, read any book with a picture of a granite-jawed bloke on the front.

It was at this point that Marian took a male name and, funnily enough, decided on 'George' after her bloke. She took the name 'Eliot' because it was 'a good mouth-filling word'. I've repeated it over and over and I still feel hungry.

# 'George got called a harlot, which in some women's eyes would be an improvement on horseface'

After George wrote *The Mill On The Floss*, she became very successful. George and George became popular with nobs and literary types, and although George (woman) wasn't much of a looker (see pictures), men were enthralled by her. Henry James, the writer, said of her, 'Yes, behold me literally in love with this great horse-faced blue stocking'. Some compliment!

In *Daniel Deronda*, George Eliot wrote, 'We women are brought up to look like flowers, to look as pretty as we can and be dull without complaining. This is my notion about plants. They are often bored and that is the reason some of them have got poisonous'. Talk to them folks!

George Lewes died in 1878 and George E. was devastated. Well, for a bit. Eighteen months later she managed to get herself together enough to marry one Johnny Cross who was twenty years her junior. Nothing like a bit of young flesh to banish the memory of your old man. George and Johnny went to Italy together. George looked better, happier and younger and no doubt she felt very worthy and not a bit sinful. Johnny, however, went bonkers and plunged from the window of their hotel into the Grand Canal. It led to a lot of rumours about George's sexual appetite. No-one investigated the possibility that Johnny was pissed and fell out. Then again, they weren't on an 18/30 holiday — more like a 40/60 holiday. George got called a harlot, which in some women's eyes would be an improvement on horseface.

Johnny got better and they returned to London. Then, one day, George had a slight touch of laryngitis and she died four days later.

Poor old George. But she did make me suffer during English O' level with *The Mill On The Dental Twine*.

# 'Three's a bit crowded in a marriage as we know from a certain *Panorama* interview, so four is really pushing it'

# virginia woolf

was born in 1882. Her mother (gorgeous) had married (for a second time) a man called Lesley Stephen (very ungorgeous). Virginia ended up with a combination of both. As a young child she was very keen on writing and telling stories. She was a sad child, though, which could have had something to do with being sexually abused by Gerald Duckworth, her half-brother, at about the age of six.

*Virginia always had a long face on her long face*

Virginia's mother died when Virginia was thirteen, which led to her having some sort of 'breakdown'. It is difficult to find out what that means because, in those days, the stock of knowledge about mental illness could be written on the back of Cindy Crawford's personality. At that time, also, women's independence was linked with mental illness and hysteria. Sounds like the blokes had it well sewn up.

Virginia was very close to her sister, Stella, although when Stella married, it meant Virginia got a room of her own, so she wasn't too bothered when Stella left home. However, not long after her marriage, Stella died following an emergency operation. She had been pregnant and Virginia made a link between pregnancy and death and was put off men and sex.

Poor old Virginia was a very unhappy person, and, as some recent research has pointed out that roughly eighty per cent of writers are clinically depressed, it was either writing or a job in the DSS for our Virg. It is possible that Virginia had a lesbian relationship with her sister Vanessa (hardly surprising given the behaviour of her brother Mr Pervert). One of Virginia's other half-brothers, George, also came into her bedroom and made inappropriate sexual advances towards her. All in all, a family with whom Freud could have had a field day.

Virginia travelled abroad a lot after her father's death. She became ill again, hearing voices telling her to kill herself. She thought this was due to overeating and decided to starve herself. She was also convinced she had murdered her father and tried to kill herself by jumping out of a window. Her doctor had probably prescribed a husband and a pile of ironing.

## 'All in all, a family with whom Freud could have had a field day'

Virginia became obsessed with the idea of looking after a baby. The silly people she was staying with actually tried to find her one. Giving a suicidal woman a baby would have been as pointless as giving Lady Olga Maitland a position in a charity organisation.

Virginia made a living by writing articles for newspapers and teaching though she had an inheritance from her parents. Virginia's brother Thoby (I've no idea where that extra 'h' came from), began to hold soirées for his friends from Cambridge like Lytton Strachey and Leonard Woolf. This was the first Bloomsbury Group. Virginia found them all a bit stuck up.

On a journey to Greece, Virginia became physically ill and took four tumblers of champagne a day to make her better. That reminds me, must get some Special Brew for my earache. Thoby contracted

# a load of old ball crunchers

typhoid and died, probably because the offie was closed. However, the Bloomsbury Group continued to meet.

Members were very forward thinking and would discuss quite controversial subjects for the time, like semen. Not straight after dinner, though. Virginia's sister, Vanessa, married a member of the group, Clive Bell, and was quite pissed off when he and Virginia became close. Vanessa's solution to this was to try and persuade Virginia to marry. She could have saved herself time by saying, 'Keep your hands off my geezer or I'll chin you.'

Lytton Strachey considered proposing to Virginia despite the fact that he was gay. Virginia called homosexuality 'buggery' so she wouldn't have been a big hit at the annual Gay Pride March. Clive Bell declared his love for Virginia and terrible *ménage à trois*-type problems arose between Van, Virg and Clive. At this point, Virginia very sensibly wrote a novel called *The Voyage Out.*

The Bloomsbury Group liked to play pranks on people and Virginia took part in a hoax which involved the group dressing up as Abyssinians inspecting the *Dreadnought,* a secret battleship. Government officials were so stupid the prank would have

*The face of the woman who first brought the idea of 'sisterhood' to a cynical world. What a stupid, thin, pretty, doe-eyed cow*

gone undetected if the group hadn't told the Press afterwards. Not much change there then.

Virginia's eventual husband, Leonard Woolf, had been a tenant in her house. But he had always preferred her sister Vanessa. Perhaps this is a stupid idea, but could they not just have swapped husbands? Virginia and Leonard didn't fancy each other but they were good friends. They started the Hogarth Press together.

# 'Virginia called homosexuality 'buggery' so she wouldn't have been a big hit at the annual Gay Pride March'

During the war, Virginia became very disturbed and violent and had to be admitted to a nursing home. Around this time she wrote, 'Do you ever feel your life is entirely useless?'. I don't, but sometimes I feel Michael Portillo's life is.

Virginia's life was not useless, though, as she continued to produce great literature. She had an affair with the posh Vita Sackville-West but irritated her by being too intense. Posh people tend to have panic attacks if they suspect you might be about to have an emotion.

Virginia and Leonard espoused various causes. Leonard stood bail in the 'Potocki case' which centred on the publication of an obscene poem: *John Penis in the Mount of Venus*. Contrary to popular opinion, this was not written by an eight-year-old schoolboy.

Despite a very happy marriage, Virginia's depression continued to surface. In 1941, she left a suicide note and went for walk to the river, but came back because she had not weighted herself down enough. Practicalities such as this are so irritating. Sadly, Virginia rectified this

## a load of old ball crunchers

one and was successful when she tried again with stones in her pockets. I doubt I would ever try and drown myself if I felt suicidal because I am sure someone would try and harpoon me first.

# elizabeth taylor was born in Hampstead

in 1932. As a child she attended dance school and remembers having lessons with the Queen and Princess Margaret. Maybe she'd had too much sherry even then, because it's not true. Elizabeth's mother was an unsuccessful actress and her dad was gay. Perhaps not the best combination in those days for a happy well-balanced childhood.

*Liz Taylor arrives back from a fancy dress party in a distressed state at the failure of her Elton John costume*

During the Second World War, the Taylor family left for America and Tiny Taylor was dragged round film studios for screen tests. Eventually she landed a part in *Lassie Come Home* because the original star turned out to be about six inches taller than the boy star,

# a load of old ball crunchers

*Liz: 'I'm just doing this to show you that when we are married I'm not going to indulge in any of this sort of filth with you'*

Roddy Mcdowall. *Lassie* was a big box office success – maybe because we'd all like to have a dog that understands what you say and rescues people from drowning, instead of crapping on the carpet and trying to eat the next door neighbour's baby while shagging your leg.

Liz really got successful when she got a starring role in *National Velvet*, a film about a girl who disguises herself as a boy to win the Grand National. Liz reports that a fall during filming gave her a chronic back problem. As she had a stunt woman to do all the riding scenes, it seems as though the sherry intervened to cloud the old memory again.

Liz was signed to MGM studios, which had a very strict no smoking and drinking policy. Alas, Louis B. Mayer, its head, did not have a no blow-jobs from starlets policy. I don't know if Liz passed the give head stage, even though, apparently, she has very unattractive legs. Still, why that should bother men I can't imagine. The existence of a vagina is normally enough for many.

Howard Hughes, the squillionaire, was obsessed with Liz. He poured jewels all over her tummy when she was sunbathing and invited her to get 'em off. She wasn't interested though. Well, not in his jewels, anyway.

Liz began to star in some blockbuster Hollywood films, negotiating her way through various hard-ons as she went. She starred in *A Place In The Sun* with Montgomery Clift (who didn't get a hard-on because he was gay) and Shelley Winters (who didn't get a hard-on because she wasn't). Monty introduced Liz to Benzedrine (an amphetamine-like substance, not a mate of his).

I'm sorry, but it's time now to start on the husband saga. I'll be as quick as I can:

### Husband Number One: Nicky Hilton

He was the heir to the Hilton hotel chain. He was a tall, handsome, violent, alcoholic junkie and a gambler. One of his girlfriends said his penis was wider than a beer can and that making love to him was like shagging a horse. How she knew about the horse bit was never established. On their wedding night, Nicky sat in the bar all night and got pissed. Liz and Nicky fought all the

*It was technically illegal to keep your dog in a hat box, but for Liz all the rules were bent*

time so their marriage lasted about ten minutes.

# a load of old ball crunchers

**Husband Number Two: Michael Wilding** Liz met him in London while filming *Ivanhoe*. They married and moved to America. They had two kids. Michael was a bit stuffy and Liz ordered him around. Lots of women get bored with men who do exactly what they want. I don't, especially if it's shopping. At this point Liz had a couple of affairs with the hideous Victor Mature and the arrogant Frank (Immature) Sinatra. And then she met . . .

*Richard Burton spent much of his life fending off searching questions from journalists about his wife's choice of hat*

### Husband Number Three: Mike Todd

Old Mikey was a bit of a wildboy. He recorded himself and Liz nomping and gave a tape to Lord Beaverbrook. Perhaps he thought it was a Radio Four play as they are quite racy, you know. Todd was violent towards Liz but she seemed to enjoy fighting back. Move over Bruno and Tyson. In between rounds, they managed to have a daughter, Liza. Just as everything seemed all right with the marriage, Mike Todd died in a plane crash. Liz was devastated and had a breakdown. She managed to get over it by having a lot of sherry and an affair with Mike's married best friend who became . . .

### Husband Number Four: Eddie Fisher

He had been married to Debbie Reynolds, but that didn't stop old ballcruncher Taylor. She converted to Judaism and married him. She also got bored with him fairly sharpish. At this point, the bane of her life was heading towards her. She got the part as Cleopatra in the huge Hollywood disaster, which cost more than Fergie's trips abroad in the last week. Here she met . . .

### Husband Number Five: Richard Burton

Burton and Taylor fell psychotically in love. Burton used to turn up at Liz and Eddie's house drunk, demand to see Liz, tear her away from her sherry, and then snog her in front of poor old Eddie. Eddie faded into history just like a boy band after five hit singles.

## 'Liz and Burton split up, but they didn't like it and remarried. But they didn't like that either, so they split up again. This could have gone on until they both died'

By now, Liz was becoming a bit silly and starrish. It was written into her contract that she did not have to appear on set if she had her period. Some poor sod was employed for the express purpose of checking her knickers. The silly woman needed a slap and a handful of Feminax if you ask me. Liz was denounced by the Vatican, but went ahead and married Burton. They pissed it up round the world for the next

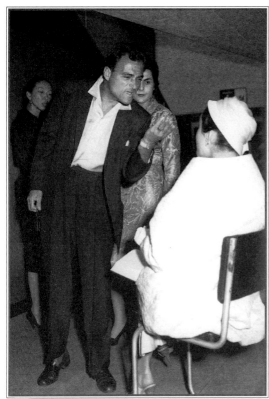

*Liz auditions another potential husband, seen here attempting the very difficult 'what time do you call this, where's my dinner' section.*

few years. Despite the fact that they were madly in love, Burton still managed to get his leg over other beauties a few times. So clever the way men can do both isn't it? So, Liz and Burton split up, but they didn't like it and remarried. But they didn't like that either, so they split up again. This could have gone on until they both died, but it didn't because Liz met...

### Husband Number Six: John Warner

He was a Republican politician and Liz did everything she could for his career by supporting the democrats at certain functions. At this point Liz was eating loads. At last she'd got her priorities right! Despite the tremendous attractions of Republican political life, like meeting Mr and Mrs Braindead, the Reagans, Liz didn't like political life. And so they divorced. By this time Liz had poured so much booze and drugs down her gullet, a trip to the Betty Ford Celebrity Withdrawal Hotel was inevitable. On her second visit, Liz met . . .

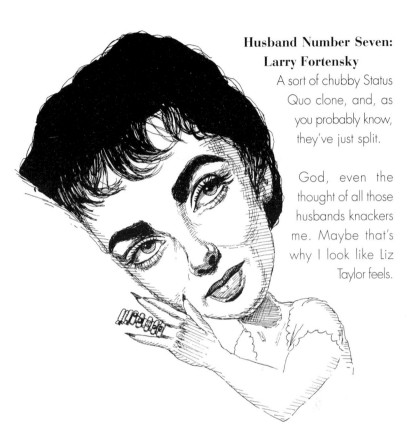

**Husband Number Seven:
Larry Fortensky**
A sort of chubby Status
Quo clone, and, as
you probably know,
they've just split.

God, even the
thought of all those
husbands knackers
me. Maybe that's
why I look like Liz
Taylor feels.

# emily brontë

Had Emily Brontë been around today, she would have been a Goth. She was a dark, brooding rock-n-roll chick, who would have been quite at home at a Cure gig.

Emily was born in 1818 at Thornton in Yorkshire and had three older sisters, Maria, Elizabeth and Charlotte, and a brother, Branwell. She also had a younger sister, Anne. Emily's father was a very strict clergyman who ministered to a church in Howarth. The family lived in a stone house built at top of very steep, cobbled hill, next to a graveyard, and beyond it there were paths to the moors. Hardly a Barrett home in Torquay and the perfect setting for writing passionate novels about ghosts and mad blokes.

Emily's mother died when she was three and the children's father sent Maria, Elizabeth, Charlotte and Emily to a school for daughters of the clergy. If this had been a happy experience, it's possible Emily might have cheered up and started listening to a bit of Right Said Fred, but it was the school from hell. You can get some idea of it from reading *Jane Eyre* by Charlotte, although, had Emily written it, there'd have been a few more bats and the odd ghost. The founder of the school believed in harsh discipline and unremitting

*My publisher's research dept pull out all the stops with an artist's impression of what Emily would have looked like after thirty cans of Special Brew and a visit to a tattooist in Easterhouse*

work. Best days of your life? Bollocks. Not only was the regime cruel, but the food was dreadful and the place was freezing in the winter. (I've been to restaurants like that in South London.) Maria and Elizabeth died of TB and typhoid broke out at the school so Charlotte and Emily went home.

# 'Emily stayed at home as housekeeper and had to make do with daydreaming about heathen men chasing her over the moors'

At home, the Brontë children educated themselves and wrote adventures set in imaginary lands. Emily and Anne had their own fantasy world called Gondal. I suppose it would have been quite hard to write anything interesting about living with a vicar. Interesting, randy vicars didn't really get going until the *Sun* invented them in the seventies.

*Coping with toothache and wearing big hats presented many problems for the Brontë sisters*

Emily went back to school when she was seventeen but again pined for home. She had got used to her isolated life and was shy and awkward in company. The Howarth Women's Assertiveness Group only had two members and they were bolshy sheep. She became a teacher in Halifax as all the girls had to earn money for Branwell's education. Why pray, I hear you ask? Because, dear friends, Branwell was the proud owner of testicles and they came first in England in the nineteenth century.

The sisters thought of setting up a school together but decided to improve their own education first and went to a pensionnat in Belgium. (At least they might have had some nice chocolate there.) While they were in Belgium, their aunt, who was looking after their father, died rather inconveniently, and they had to come home. Emily stayed at home as housekeeper and had to make do with daydreaming about heathen men chasing her over the moors. Charlotte returned for a bit because she was in love with her tutor but he wasn't interested so she came back again and had to make do with dreaming up Mr Rochester. So much more satisfying than the real thing anyway.

## 'Branwell was the proud owner of testicles and they came first in England in the nineteenth century'

They tried to set up a school but couldn't get any pupils. Unfortunately no-one could read the ad in the local paper. One of the greatest problems that the Brontë sisters had was Branwell's behaviour. He got drunk every night at the pub down the road and was addicted to opium. More of a Sex Pistols fan then. Enough money was scraped together for Branwell to go to art college in London. Art colleges were very different then. These days, being an alcoholic drug addict should go to the top of the old CV for a place at art school. Branwell set off to London, went up a couple of steps of the art college, decided he didn't want to go, got drunk for a week and then came home again. Bet he got a lovely welcome from the sisters that had paid for his drinking binge in London.

# 'They decided to take men's names as they knew that if people found out they were women they would pooh pooh the poetry and wipe their bottoms on it'

Emily, meanwhile, had been beavering away in her room writing poetry, except it wasn't the kind of poetry you write when you're fifteen and your mum won't let you buy an underwired bra, it was dark and passionate. Charlotte discovered Emily's poems and thought she should publish them. They decided to take men's names as they knew that if people found out they were women they would pooh pooh the poetry and wipe their bottoms on it. So Emily became Ellis Bell. The poetry was published and then Emily wrote *Wuthering Heights*. (A girl at our school, who hadn't even read it, rather charmingly renamed it Wuthering Huts during an exam . . . she failed.) Lots of critics have been a bit snobbish about *Wuthering Heights* (especially after Kate Bush sang a song about being let in at the window and even more especially now that Cliff Richard is starring in a musical version), but it can't be beaten if you want a really good read with unrequited love, ghosts, death, lots of shouting and a hero who would be well worth a jump. (Incidentally, he's not a bit like HeathCliff Richard and there's no songs.)

Branwell died in 1848 and Emily caught a cold at his funeral which developed into TB. She refused any medical aid and carried on with household duties until she died. So, not only did he take all her money for an aborted assault on art college, the bastard killed her as well.

# a load of old ball crunchers

When I was an adolescent I wanted to be Emily Brontë. Then I found out she loved walking on the moors. Stuff that!

# mary wollstonecraft was born in

Spitalfields in London in 1759. She wasn't much of a looker and, in those days, that meant a bit of a future husband problem. She had a brother, Ned, who was very spoilt, and throughout her childhood she felt that no-one was interested in her. Already a chip was starting to form on her shoulder. Nothing wrong with that. I love chips and they get things done.

When Mary's grandfather died, he left Ned a third of his will and the girls in the family got nothing. I'd have found it hard not to go and jump up and down on his grave. The family moved to a farm in Epping which failed and then on to another one in Yorkshire. Mary was a solitary child. Her dad was a drunk and Mary was constantly called upon to shield her mother from his blows. By this time, the chip was so big, hopefully, he got a mouthful of potato.

By the age of fifteen, Mary was a harsh critic of her parents' social attitudes. The family moved back to London and Mary became friendly with a local couple, the Clares, who were about her only friends. They introduced her to someone called Fanny Blood to whom she became very close. Mary eventually had to get a job and, in those days, there wasn't much on offer, so she became a companion to a Mrs

*False hairpieces were somewhat unsophisticated in the eighteenth century*

Dawson in Bath; a job the writer Fanny Burney called 'toad eating'. (Still, always the chance of being left a bit of money if the old dear croaked, arf, arf.)

After Mary's mother died, she went to live with the Bloods. The family were a bit like Wayne and Waynetta Slob. Always broke, cramped and messy. Mary supported them for much of her life. Mary's sister, Eliza, married a geezer called Meredith Bishop and, after having a baby, had one of those ubiquitous 'we-don't-know-anything-about-psychiatry-in-the-eighteenth-century' breakdowns. Mary persuaded Eliza to creep out of the house without the baby and set up home near Hackney. They took false names. The baby died and Eliza blamed Mary. Bit more serious than borrowing her silk blouse without telling her.

# 'In those days of no antibiotics and mice up your jacksie while you slept, many people died young'

Mary moved to Newington and tried to set up a village school. Fanny, meanwhile, had gone off to Lisbon to marry her fiancé and was pregnant. When Fanny was due to give birth, Mary went out there. Both mother and child died. Mary must have thought she was a jinx by this point, but, to be fair, in those days of no antibiotics and mice up your jacksie while you slept, many people died young.

Back in England, Mary began to write and produced *Thoughts on The Education of Daughters*, full of pretty radical views for that period. (Just can't stop talking about periods, sorry.) Mary then went to Ireland to become governess to the daughters of Viscount Kingsborough. The Viscount felt free to make advances to Mary because he was rich and a bloke and his wife was knackered having produced twelve children. Mary left the job in disgrace after a row with the Viscount's wife. You didn't need to do much to wind up rich people in those days. Breathing was normally enough.

At twenty-eight, Mary found herself jobless and in debt. As social security hadn't been invented she had to try and find some sucker to support her. She turned to Joseph (Sucker) Johnson, her publisher, who set her up in a flat. Mary became obsessed with a friend of Johnson's called Fuseli. He was a bit of a goth who liked pornography and liked shocking Mary. Unfortunately for Mary, he had a wife.

Mary then wrote *Vindication of the Rights of Man* which demonstrated her sympathy for the poor. She followed this up with *Vindication of the Rights of Women* and became quite famous, although she had a lot of critics. One of these was a git called Bentham who thought women should not have the vote because they are:

*Mary looking a bit boss-eyed here... must be from her 'Disorder of the Bowels' period*

1) Easily distracted from political thought.
2) Economically dependent on men.
3) Ill-educated.
4) Not in need of the vote because of man's sexual dependence on them.
5) Liable to cause domestic strife.

Oh dear, he forgot to say we are complete fluffy little wabbits who don't have a single independent thought in our heads.

# a load of old ball crunchers

One of Mary's points in her pamphlet about women is that society encourages women to be obsessed with their looks and trivia of a domestic kind. Thank God it's not like that now.

## 'The Viscount felt free to make advances to Mary because he was rich and a bloke and his wife was knackered'

At the age of thirty-three Mary was at the peak of her success. She tarted herself up and went off to France for a bit. She was still whacko over Fuseli, who was still not interested. But Mary felt she had to see him every day because of their mental affinity and asked his wife if she could move in with the two of them. Not surprisingly, his wife went berserk and told her to get out. Poor old Mary, the chip started to expand again. Lots of women repeat the pattern of unsuccessful relationships and Mary was no exception. In France, she met an American army captain, Gilbert Imlay, had an affair with him and, like you did in those days, got pregnant. All her friends hated Gilbert and one was so horrible about him, Mary got a disorder of the bowels. Mary had a little girl whom she called Fanny. Gilbert had lost interest by this time and Mary began to feel suicidal.

Back in London, she tried to drown herself but couldn't make herself sink. (I had no idea it was this difficult to drown.) She suggested to Gilbert she move in with him and his new woman (obviously she was on for a threesome), but that went down like a glass of urine (i.e. not well, unless you're Sarah Miles), so she moved on.

Mary did eventually find a teeny bit of happiness with William Godwin, a philosopher. He had quite a few women after him and, despite the fact that one turned down his proposal of marriage, when he asked, Mary agreed. Still, soiled goods are better than no goods. Mary became pregnant, but during the birth failed to expel the placenta properly, which became septic. The doctor tried to get it out by hand, which must have been a very unpleasant experience just after you've had a baby. Unfortunately, he was unsuccessful and Mary died, which is an even more unpleasant experience.

# mata hari's real name was Margarethe Gertrude Zelle

and she was born in Holland. Her other siblings were blonde and blue-eyed, whereas Gertie was very dark, leading people to suspect that Mrs Zelle might have been playing the field. Gertie's mum died when Gertie was fourteen and she went off to a training school for teachers. She didn't do much work at this place and got round it by flirting outrageously with the teachers. I tried this when I forgot my plimsolls, but as I was only five, the sports master wasn't impressed.

*Mata was famed for her 'elegant swanlike neck'. In order to be incognito, she therefore had it surgically removed*

After Gertie left the training school, nothing is known of her movements for the next eighteen months, but it is thought she went into a convent. Wonder how her flirting technique worked on the nuns?

When Gertie was eighteen, in 1895, she answered an ad in a paper for a wife, placed by a friend of a Captain Rudolph McCleod as a practical joke. What was more of a joke was that they actually got engaged in six days. Gertie's drunkard of a dad was not keen but they obviously topped him up with a bit of cider and he agreed. Captain Rudolph was Dutch, but Gertie didn't wear his cap when they were doing the business, because she got pregnant and had a little boy. For some unfathomable reason, they called this poor child Norman.

Captain Rudolph returned with his family to Java and Gertie had a second child, a girl whom she called Juana. Flirty Gertie was very popular with the young officers and the captain didn't like it, so in a jealous huff he arranged to be transferred to Sumatra, where he thought there would be less officers. When Gertie arrived with the kids, he noticed they had been seriously neglected but didn't make an issue of it. However, whilst in Sumatra, poor old Norman almost died, leading people to suspect he had been poisoned. Eventually, a native employee confessed she had done it because the captain had mistreated her husband. Good job that's not the fashion over here or the children of government ministers would be dropping like flies. Juana had very sensibly refused the bad food so she was unharmed. Poor old Norman, the gannet, had made the biggest mistake of his life for a bit of dinner. But I can sympathise with that.

# 'Poor old Norman had made the biggest mistake of his life for a bit of dinner. But I can sympathise with that'

Rather predictably, Gertie and the captain's marriage went downhill and they returned to Holland and separated. The captain got custody, so Gertie decided to try and make her fortune in Paris where the streets are paved with gold American Express cards. Gertie tried and failed to get acting work, so decided to pose as an artist's model. The artist wanted to do her starkers, but Gertie would only agree to it if his wife was present. I wouldn't have agreed even if his entire extended family were there.

# a load of old ball crunchers

*Some kids like to experiment by dressing up in their parent's old curtains. Unfortunately Mata never got out of the habit*

The artist told Gertie her breasts were flabby and pendulous. They don't beat about the bush these French artists, do they? Gertie then worked as a prostitute, because men desperate for a shag aren't that bothered about the dimensions of your chest. She returned briefly to Holland to slag off her husband to his cousin, thus ruining her chances of being set up in a house by the cousin. Still, who wants to stay in a house in Holland, when you can waggle your flabby pendulous breasts around running for buses in London or Paris?

Gertie returned to Paris where she became 'Mata Hari' which means 'Flabby, Pendulous One'. . . no, all right, it means 'Eye Of The Morning'.

As Mata Hari, she became a striptease artiste and performed sensual dances of the East. She invented a complete history for Mata Hari with lots of inconsistencies and no mention of poor old Norman and Juana. Mata Hari became a huge success. Her snake dance was something to behold. Her chameleon dance wasn't quite so great though because no-one could see it.

# 'Gertie returned to Paris where she became "Mata Hari" which means "Flabby, Pendulous One"...'

In 1914, Mata Hari was spotted in the company of the Berlin Chief of Police and it was presumed from this that she was employed in the German Secret Service. This seems a bit unfair as she could have just been asking him the way to the nearest Ladies. Mata worked in Amsterdam for a while and was employed by an impresario who was putting on a performance of the opera *Lucia Di Lammermoor*. He thought he could liven it up with a bit of Mata's exotic dancing. The show closed after one night. This impresario is obviously an ancestor of the one who thinks Cliff Richard makes a good Heathcliff.

At this point, Mata Hari was being followed around by the French Secret Service. When they accused her of being a German spy, she offered to

*Early versions of the tampon were a little bit too big to fit most women comfortably*

# a load of old ball crunchers

work for them as well. I wonder how easy it is to work undercover if you are a striptease artiste?

Eventually, after bobbing about round Europe, Mata was lured back to Paris. She was arrested while she was having her breakfast – a box of chocolates. Probably not as good for your bowels as Allbran, but more interesting than a bowl of dry brown twigs that tastes like dry brown twigs.

Mata was tried on a count of six

charges, one being that she gave information to the Germans about a new chemical ink discovery. Not exactly high-powered poison umbrella in the thigh stuff is it?

Mata was found guilty and sentenced to death. The three nuns looking after her in prison went to the execution site with her and Mata jokingly told one to get out of the way or she would be shot. Not the greatest joke of all time, but I suppose when you're about to be riddled with bullets, it's not easy to think of good one-liners.

# 17

# elizabeth I

was two years and eight months old when she lost her mother and her mother lost her head. Her mother was Anne Boleyn, one of Henry VIII's unfortunate wives. Elizabeth was in an equally precarious position, being heir to the throne and in danger of being plotted out of the running. This was why she was kept away from court during her childhood.

*The Virgin Queen or Norman Tebbit in drag?*

At the age of eighteen, Elizabeth got more of a grip. She had her own townhouse and her own income, but she couldn't do what most eighteen-year-olds would do and spend money on beer and trash the house.

Elizabeth was plagued by migraine throughout her life, perhaps explaining why she was called the Virgin Queen, because every time the chance of a seeing-to came up, she had the headache.

Other headaches included her elder Catholic sister, Mary, and the Duke of Northumberland who was plotting to get Lady Jane Grey on the throne. Lady Jane Grey was proclaimed rightful heir when Edward, Henry's only son, died. Mary wasn't happy with this and saw her chance when the Duke of Northumberland's supporters started quarrelling amongst themselves. Lady Jane got the chop. She had only been queen for nine days. It's a lot longer than I've ever lasted on a diet though and that seemed about nine years. Eventually, Mary was proclaimed queen. She was betrothed to Philip of Spain and amused herself by sending people to the Tower of London. Horrible place, but a nice view of Tower Bridge.

# 'Elizabeth was plagued by migraine throughout her life, perhaps explaining why she was called the Virgin Queen'

At the age of twenty-five, when Mary snuffed it, Elizabeth became Queen. One of her favourite men at court was Robert Dudley, whose first wife, Amy Robsart, had fallen down the stairs and broken her neck. The verdict on this was accidental death, although many people assumed Robert had been involved. Amy may have done it herself in Princess Diana-style when she found out about her rival, although there is no record of her throwing herself at a cabinet.

When Elizabeth became queen, she had all the old coins melted down to make new ones. Unfortunately, the fumes badly affected the workers. The advice given to make themselves better was to drink from human skulls. The sad bastards fell for it and most of them died.

In 1562, Elizabeth got smallpox, always a dodgy illness because you tended to end up looking like the Singing Detective afterwards. Elizabeth didn't believe the doctor's diagnosis and told him to get out. However, she realised the illness was serious and sent for him again. His pride was wounded and he refused to come, but a knife pressed against his ribs encouraged him to make the right decision. If only I could do that with the locum at my local surgery life would be so much easier.

Meanwhile, Robert Dudley, by now The Earl Of Leicester (potential shags were always promoted), was proposed as a possible husband for Mary Queen of Scots. Not a good choice as far as old pox face was concerned. She need not have worried because Darnley nipped up and married her without the queen's permission.

All Elizabeth's advisers were desperate to marry her off and pestered her day and night to get herself a bloke. This resulted in temper tantrums, during which Elizabeth would swear at them using such naughty terms as

*It's a wonder men in Elizabethan times ever got off with anyone when you look at the state of them*

'God's blood' and 'God's wounds!'. In those days, that kind of swearing by a woman was quite something, though, as all the other women said things like, 'Oh dear', and then blushed a lot.

## 'Lady Jane got the chop. She had only been queen for nine days. It's a lot longer than I've ever lasted on a diet though and that seemed about nine years'

# a load of old ball crunchers

Elizabeth was fending off continuous plots, and by the age of thirty-nine she is supposed to have been raddled and covered in make-up. She had an advantage over the rest of us, though, because she was the queen and could get any bloke she liked, even though she was doing a passable impression of Alice Cooper.

Dudley secretly married a woman called Lettice Devereux, a widow, and Elizabeth really went into one. She ordered him to be put into his own special tower. Ah! She must have really loved him. Dudley feigned illness and Elizabeth went rushing straight to his bedside. Why, oh why, oh why are we women so gullible?

Potential spotty royal husbands were still being lined up like a queue for Clearasil at Boots. One who nearly made it was the Duke of Alencon from the House of Valois. He was twenty-three and Elizabeth was forty-six. However, for a change, the advisers weren't enthusiastic. Everyone tried to talk Elizabeth out of it but she would have none of it. It was left to her ladies in waiting to have a crack and they took the, 'he's riddled with disease' line. Elizabeth finally gave in. It must have reminded her of her dad, Henry, who was a clap clinic's delight. The Duke cried, but it was to no avail, Elizabeth remained a spinster.

*This is Essex Man. Essex girls go on shagfrenzy as soon as they get up town. I rest my case*

Another favourite geezer of Elizabeth's was Walter Raleigh and the legend most people know about him is that he threw his cloak down in a puddle so Elizabeth could avoid getting her feet wet.

Evidently, this is not true, and if this is the only story they can muster about him, he must have been a bit of a saddo.

Plotting continued apace and eventually Elizabeth had to sign a warrant for Mary Queen of Scots' execution because she just didn't seem to be able to give up trying to get on the throne of England. When Mary was executed, Elizabeth was very upset. Not so the population of London. They danced in the streets in their usual, sensitive, 'We love looking at horrible car accidents' sort of way.

The Spanish Armada, originally intended to come and save Mary, got there a bit late. Elizabeth gave a rousing speech down at Tilbury which contained the famous words, 'I have the body of a weak and feeble woman, but I have the heart and stomach of a king'. (Hopefully, she didn't have the stomach of Henry VIII.)

The Earl of Essex also became a favourite, but he behaved like a naughty boy, secretly marrying, not doing as he was told in Ireland, turning his back on the Queen, and calling her a king in petticoats. He waved goodbye to his head, too.

Elizabeth lived to a ripe old age compared to most people in those days. They lived to a ripe young age, because everyone was riddled with disease and you could smell them coming a couple of miles off. Maybe she was a virgin queen after all.

# 18

# marie curie

was born Marie Sklodovska in Warsaw and was a bit of a swat. She got a gold medal at school, which is a bit more impressive than the stars we used to get that cost about 50p for a packet of two hundred. When she was young she was a bit overweight and the other kids called her names. So she thought, I'll show them. I felt the same way too, but I didn't show them by getting two Nobel Prizes (not yet anyway).

Marie's first job was as a governess with a horrible and stupid rich family, whom she said were 'demoralised by wealth', which I suppose is a nicer way of saying they were a bunch of upper class arseholes who deserved the French Revolution treatment. So Marie moved on to another family miles away from home. She still thought everyone in the family was stupid but they were much nicer to her.

Marie secretly taught Polish to the locals (who were under the yoke of the Russians at the time) – so politically her heart was in the right place. So was her

*Journal entry #57: 'I have discovered either a Cure for Cancer, or an entirely new form of Gooseberry Preserve. It is now in the hands of God'*

nose because she thought they were really smelly, not an ideologically sound opinion really.

At this point Marie's weight problem had sorted itself out hormonally and she had become quite pretty. The oldest son of the family, who naturally had not looked at her twice before because she was Lard Woman, very predictably fell in love with her and asked her to marry him. Suddenly, the family who had treated her like one of them, treated her like one of the Addams family. So Marie left that job. On the train journey home she reports that although people were very friendly to her, she did not return their friendship in case she had to give them some of her food. Mean, but ultimately, sensible.

# 'Marie learnt to cook and how to have sex because she became pregnant. The scientific formula for this in case you're interested is:

## Male Genitals + Female Genitals - Contraception = Up the Duff'

Marie's sister, Bronya, offered to let her come and live with her in Paris and Marie signed up at the Sorbonne. Marie was having quite a good time going out to the theatre and to balls. When her father found out, he wrote to her and told her to stop. Now, if my father had written to me from hundreds of miles away and told me to stop, I would

# a load of old ball crunchers

have just carried on and sent him a nice postcard saying I was in every night, working. Not so our Marie. She even moved out of her sister's house so she could avoid the hectic social life and dedicate herself to work. This was a big mistake because she had no money and didn't even know how to make soup. It didn't even occur to her to blowtorch a couple of turnips with a Bunsen Burner. She survived on bread and butter and cups of tea. Many students living on the oh-so-generous government grant will identify with this. Apparently these days, some students even eat dog food. Not very nourishing, but their hair looks nice and shiny.

At this point Marie was collapsing from malnourishment, but, despite the career possibilities this opened as a potential supermodel, she accepted a couple of lamb chops from her sister and soldiered on.

Then she met Pierre Curie, who was a French scientist. They fell in love and got married. Marie learnt to cook and how to have sex because she became pregnant. The scientific formula for this in case you're interested is:

Male Genitals + Female Genitals - Contraception = Up the Duff

*'This looks far too small to get so... in. Good job I can't make it then'*

Marie went straight back to the laboratory after the birth of her child and began concentrating on what she was to become famous for. At that time a scientist called Becquerel had observed the phenomenon of radioactivity and the race was on to discover if there was a new element.

Marie's daughter remarks that Marie had 'a marvellous feminine curiosity'. (Although this didn't extend to the recipe for soup obviously.) Marie and Pierre spent their time looking through tons of pitchblende to isolate the new element they were convinced existed. Well, I suppose it beats watching paint dry by a short head.

Eventually they were successful and named the new element polonium after Poland. Marie's daughter remarks that at this stage Marie had actually learnt how to cook as there is a recipe in the margin of her scientific notes for gooseberry preserve. So arose the completely new educational discipline of domestic science.

## 'Marie went on to win the Nobel prize for physics and later the Nobel prize for chemistry. Sadly there was not a Nobel prize for gooseberry preserve or she would have got that too'

Not content with discovering polonium, the Curies found another new element and called it radium – after Radland I suppose. At this point, they had very little money and all their experiments were conducted in a shed in the garden. Although they found it difficult to see, both of them probably glowed in the dark by now, making their work a bit easier.

Marie went on to win the Nobel prize for physics and later the Nobel prize for chemistry. Sadly, there was not a Nobel prize for gooseberry preserve or she would have got that too. Some housewife in France got the Nobel prize for soup.

Marie was starting to become famous at this point which of course meant more money and a welcome move out of the shed into a proper laboratory. She wrote books and was responsible for the Curie Foundation – a make-up which went on very smoothly and gave you a glowing complexion.

Marie was now unstoppable. She went on a couple of tours of America, became Chief of Work in Physics at the Sorbonne, and realised that being able to make soup wasn't such a big deal after all. Sadly, Pierre was killed in an accident and after this Marie became a pitiful and incurably lonely woman. Her daughter says she did not find happiness again, but learned to love the little joys of daily life. I don't know what the little joys of life were to Marie, but, to me, anything little is not that joyful.

Marie died at the age of sixty-seven of radiation poisoning (nothing like suffering for your art). She retains her glowing reputation as one of the most famous and respected scientists although not a keen eater of bread and butter.

# lady hamilton

All the nice girls love a sailor, apparently. However, Lady Hamilton, according to the morals of the age, was not a nice girl because she played the field.

Lady Hamilton was born Emily Lyon near Chester in 1765. Her dad died when she was a year old and she and her mum moved back in with her grandma. I suppose after being brought up with two women you'd be keen to get out and have a bit of a seeing-to. In 1779, Emily's mother got work in London. It is not known what Emily's mum's job was, but Emily, who had become Emma by now, became an undernursemaid to a surgeon called Doctor Budd. I don't think she was under Dr Budd, but she managed to get under quite a lot of blokes at that time, including a captain who she slept with to save a relative from a press gang. She got the nickname 'Patroness of The Navy' which tells us she had piped aboard quite a few sailors.

*ma tries to get into RADA with substandard mime. The selectors ve failed to realise she is not a ee but a traffic warden*

Emma also worked at Dr Graham's Temple of Health, a sort of eighteenth century health farm. Dr Graham was a bit of a Casanova who liked jumping into the mud bath with naked girls. In fact, the whole place seems to have been designed to satisfy his sexual needs. There was a Celestial Bed which improved fertility for example. (Pull the other one Dr Graham.)

# a load of old ball crunchers

Emma met a Sir Harry Fetherstonehaugh (pronounced 'Shaganythingthatmoves'), and he took her to his Sussex estate, where Emma followed his lead and slept with all his friends. Sir Harry sent Emma away when she got pregnant and she was set up in a house in

*Emma holds her pose for the artist, even when a twenty-four foot pigeon flies overhead*

London by a geezer called Greville – a bit of a goody-goody she had tempted into bed. (How hard is it to tempt a goody-goody into bed? Let me refer you to the Catholic Church.)

Greville sent Emma to the painter George Romney, because she was gorgeous and he wanted some pictures of her. Obviously not as effective as photographs but at least Greville didn't get his pictures back with the head cut off. George Romney had left his wife and kids at home in Cumberland, intending to return when he had made a bit of money. So far, this had taken fifteen years, so no wonder his wife moaned that he never did the washing up.

Through Greville, Emma met Sir William Hamilton who was the British ambassador in Naples and a widower. Emma went out to visit, and, naturally, she ended up in bed with Sir William. She was also a big hit with the king of Naples, Ferdinand. He had the common touch and ate pasta with his hands. Emma didn't sleep with him, though. It's a bit off-putting having bolognaise smeared all over you in the sack.

Emma began to entertain people with classical poses. This meant she used to stand in a series of positions dressed in an old sheet. In those days people thought it was great, for some reason. Emma married Sir William, but it was destined not to last as he was quite old and also some bloke called Nelson was heading for Naples. Nelson and Emma didn't get together until he had lost an eye and an arm. In fact he was more of a half-Nelson by then but still a jolly good shag, obviously. He conveniently managed to lose his wife and his stepchild and he and Em got together. Both were exhibitionists seeking glory. Nelson didn't do poses though, because he couldn't hold the sheet properly – indeed, neither was he very good at putting on duvet covers.

# 'I suppose after being brought up with two women you'd be keen to get out and have a bit of a seeing-to'

It's strange that Emma and Nelson actually didn't get together until they were both a bit raddled. Emma, who had been a stunning beauty, was beginning to get past it in her thirties and looked a bit of a wreck. As you probably know, though, Nelson liked a wreck so he didn't mind. Sir William Hamilton was replaced as ambassador in Naples and recalled to London with Nelson. Emma was very keen to travel home by land to show off at various courts in Europe.

Emma became pregnant with Nelson's child and called the baby Horatia. Poor kid, what a dreadful name. She was the Zowie Bowie of her day. Still, it's better than Oceanus or Columbus which I'm told are still doing the rounds. Emma began to put on loads of weight doing a bit of comfort eating while Nelson was away blasting ships out of

# a load of old ball crunchers

the water. Even when he was away, Nelson was very bossy and tried to rule Emma's life. He didn't manage to prevent the frequent ingestion of bacon sandwiches, though. Nelson, as you know from occasionally looking up from your copy of *Jackie* during history lessons, was killed at the Battle of Trafalgar. Emma indulged in a fair bit of theatrical grief, using the 'Oh dear my bloke's just been killed in a battle' pose.

Once she had lost Nelson, Emma was in a bit of trouble. She tried to get off with the Duke of Queensberry, who was in his eighties, but he wasn't keen on bacon sandwiches. Or marriage – you know blokes! He probably reckoned he still had a bit more bed-hopping to do.

Emma was in huge debt. The bill from the pork pie shop ran into millions. She managed to hold off her creditors for two years, but eventually was forced to live in what was known as a spunging house, a place where broke people had to live near a prison. I recently put in a request to live in a Victoria sponging house, a place where fat people live near a bakers, but had no joy.

Big Emma was eventually smuggled out of England disguised as Bernard Manning and lived on Turkey Roast in France. However, there she became an alcoholic and died a pauper at the age of fifty-one. Still, better to die drunk than sober, I say.

## 'Nelson and Emma didn't get together until he had lost an eye and an arm. In fact he was more of a half-Nelson by then'

# emmeline pankhurst didn't

really come into her own until her husband Richard had snuffed it, but he is worth mentioning because he shaped her political views to some extent. He was called The Red Doctor, because he was a leftie, although he did have red hair too. Unfortunately, he had a squeaky voice like Emlyn Hughes, so when he spoke on behalf of Labour, everyone voted Conservative.

Doctor Pankhurst pushed Emmeline's political interests and prescribed reading for her. What a marvellous man, you might think. How liberal in the Victorian age to teach his wife about politics. Then you find he left the domestic chores to Emmeline as well. New man becomes ancient man yet again.

*Even in her eighties, Emmeline tried to wind policemen up with her famous suffragette sideways stare*

The Pankhursts had three daughters; Christabel, Sylvia and Adela – a ready-formed feminist hit-squad. At this point in history women were beginning to assert themselves. A big scandal blew up in my home town, Camberwell in London, at the time, because there was a woman there who wore trousers. Men started to panic in case women fancied wearing their pants too and discovered what ridiculous, hideous contraptions they were.

Doctor Pankhurst wasn't having much luck in local elections. It didn't help that the Tories were paying people to get pissed and disrupt his speeches. These days they just get pissed themselves and do it. Added to this insult, the Tories were accusing Doctor Pankhurst of being unChristian. They appear still to have their own form of Christianity. It's called 'Not Being Christian In Any Shape Or Form'. Emmeline was very angry about the treatment her husband got and wrote to a judge about it, but was ignored. How unusual for a judge not to listen to anyone with a genuine case. Maybe she should have burgled some houses, got herself shot at and then applied for legal aid.

## 'The Tories appear still to have their own form of Christianity. It's called "Not Being Christian In Any Shape Or Form"'

Instead, the Pankhursts opened a shop which didn't do very well. Maybe a women's trousers shop was a little premature. They rented what is now the Russell Hotel in London. This was a house with a huge number of rooms and Emmeline probably didn't have time to do anything except hoover. She must have been relieved when the lease ran out and they were forced to move to Cheshire. Doctor Pankhurst didn't move there immediately, he went off somewhere to sort out his gastric ulcers. Gastric ulcers are caused by stress and the sound of all that hoovering can't have helped.

By now, Emmeline was knackered and would sometimes stay in bed for days on end with a hot water bottle. Just imagine, our heroine could have avoided all that work by not getting up. Sorry girls, we haven't got the vote, Mrs Pankhurst fancied a kip.

But, eventually, Emmeline got up and joined the Independent Labour Party. She was determined to keep up her personal standards and saw no reason to dress badly just because she was a socialist. I see no reason to dress well just because I am a fat person and we're supposed to make the best of ourselves.

# 'Maybe a women's trousers shop was a little premature'

Doctor Pankhurst stood as Labour party candidate in Gorton and lost. He was stoned by stoned young Tories. The sophistication of political debate has improved somewhat these days though. Look how adult everyone is at Prime Minister's question time in the House of Commons.

Emmeline, conversely, was very popular. She was a good speaker and, unlike her husband, didn't sound like a mouse being put through a mangle. Emmeline pushed for reforms. She wanted the poor treated better and improved prisons. We could do with her today.

Whilst Emmeline and her daughter were away in Geneva, poor old Dr Pankhurst died. The children were not in for a happy time as, because of Emmeline's views, they were attacked at school. It seems a bit unfair that the behaviour of the parents should be taken out on the kids, unless they're William and Harry.

*Getting lifted by the Old Bill again. Note that in those days there was no youth culture, so Mods tended t be in their fifties and sixties*

Emmeline formed The Womens Social and Political Union in an attempt to try and get votes for women. She and other women were fed up with all the men taking the piss out of them in the Commons. Jokes were made about having a pregnant Prime Minister. Of course, since then we have had a Prime Minister who has been pregnant, with the Devil unfortunately.

The women's polite protest wasn't working very well so they decided it was time to become more radical. They declared war which was a lot more exciting than handing out cucumber sandwiches. The women went to various political meetings and asked question after question about votes for women. They were dragged out and beaten. I don't remember anyone doing that to Maggie – shame!

The WSPU also heckled Churchill who had initially supported them. The reaction was similar. They were slapped, pinched and beaten with umbrellas. They had dead mice and rotten vegetables thrown at them when they tried to speak. This sounds like good potential for the ingredients on Ready Steady Cook!

*Emmeline received her MBE at the same time as Yoda from* **Return of the Jedi**

Christabel took charge of the whole she-bang as she was wilder than me on Baileys Irish Cream. At the time there were various strange, feminist theories flying around. A Miss Swiney thought that sexual intercourse should only be allowed every three years. (Hold your

# a load of old ball crunchers

horses Miss Piggy, some of us quite like it.) The women continued their campaign and were in and out of prison more times than Ronnie Kray's mum. They indulged in arson and smashing windows. They also had a people's army of eighty women trained in Ju-Jitsu. I'd quite like to borrow them for a night out sometime.

When the war broke out, disagreements arose in the Pankhurst ranks. Sylvia was opposed to war, Mrs Pankhurst and Christabel weren't. They fell out. Hey sisterhood, eh?

Although the protests carried out by WSPU did actually get us women the vote, and what a great choice of things we've got to vote for – not, Mrs Pankhurst eventually stood as a Tory candidate. Makes you wish she was still around, so you could throw a few mice at her doesn't it?

# belle starr

As a child I hated Westerns and war films. Now, when I look back, I think this was because the women in them were so bloody dull. They either wept prettily, with a total absence of snot, or appeared so often carrying an apple pie, it looked like they might need surgery to remove it.

However, in the Wild West, there were some women who could shoot 'em up with the best of them. One of these was Belle Starr, who according to legend, was a sexy romantic gun totin' broad, shot through with bravado. This, I'm afraid, is an invention, because Belle Starr wasn't much to look at and wasn't a very nice person either. Of course if you looked gorgeous, you could go round shooting people to your heart's content and all you would be remembered for is that you were good todging-off fodder.

*Belle never ran from a fight. With a nineteen foot frock, she didn't walk from too many either*

Belle Starr was born Myra Shirley in 1848 in a log cabin in Missouri. When she was eight, she was sent to a young ladies' academy, where subjects like Greek and Latin were taught. Myra managed to get out of lessons because a war started on the Kansas/Missouri borders. Her father's homestead was burnt, so she managed to get out of the housework and Myra's father decided to move out of trouble to Texas, so Myra had somewhere to shop for shelves.

Myra grew up near Dallas and by the time she was eighteen, it was obvious that she was no beauty. So it was quite a good joke that she changed her name to Belle, which of course means 'beautiful' in French. (Perhaps, as she had to leave school early, she didn't realise that.)

# 'Belle had a taste for rough company and had no respect for law and order. This meant she was just like the vast majority of settlers in the Wild West'

Belle had a taste for rough company and had no respect for law and order. This meant she was just like the vast majority of settlers in the Wild West who seemed to think that the Native Americans rather liked the fact that the settlers were muscling in and grabbing land that belonged to them. Well, they didn't, and when they fought back, they were accused of being savage redskins. Still, that's wonderful American civilisation for you.

Belle met a man called Cole Younger, who rode with Jesse James. 'Riding with' in those days was a euphemism for going round on a horse shooting people and taking their money.

Cole was on the run after robbing a bank. Belle gave him shelter and I suppose as they were in the same house they thought they might as well have sex. Cole fathered Belle's first child, Pearl, although he denied this and rejected Pearl. In those days the Child Support Agency was non-existent and if you couldn't persuade a family member to chase after the offending father and pepper his backside with buckshot, there wasn't a lot you could do.

Belle decided it was easier just to get a new bloke and got together with a prospector called Jim Reed, who had a part time job as a bank and train robber. Belle and Reed and two other outlaws rode to North Canadian river country in search of gold. This involved standing in a river with a colander-type thing and sifting through lots of old pebbles in the hope that some might be yellow and shiny. This was about as interesting as a documentary about hair follicles.

Unfortunately, some poor old Native American let slip that he had $30,000 worth of gold hidden and Belle and Reed tortured him until he told them where it was. Suddenly any sympathy I had for this woman has flown out the window. Women who join in what is a predominantly male evil deserve as much sympathy as David Mellor does for his looks and dress sense.

Belle used the loot to buy some finery and return to Texas in style. She bought a velvet plumed hat, leather boots and a new six-gun. Beats splashing out at the hairdressers I suppose. She had a child by Jim, but Jim didn't last long. He was killed in a fight with one of his gang. In the Wild West most people had the life expectancy of a mayfly with a bad cold.

Belle, ever the caring role model, left her kids with her mother and rode off with a gang of horse and cattle thieves.

# a load of old ball crunchers

She got together with a Native American outlaw called Blue Duck. Native Americans give each other names which reflect their behaviour and personality. That's why I call my bloke 'Sits In Front Of Telly Farting'. Belle became the leader of the gang and masterminded all their forays over the next five years. Blue Duck was chucked in favour of a Cherokee called Sam. Sam had some influence over Belle, who was by now a hard faced twenty-eight-year-old. (I would imagine her heart wasn't too squidgy either.) Sam was one of the few men who could control Belle, and they married and lived in a cabin near Arkansas. Sounds idyllic, doesn't it? Apart from the fact they were a pair of psychos! They carried on rustling and stealing cattle and would let some of the worst bandits of the day hide out at their place. In fact, Jesse James, who was far from a big jessie, stayed for a few days. They didn't charge him any rent because he would probably have shot them if they'd tried.

> **'They married and lived in a cabin near Arkansas. Sounds idyllic, doesn't it? Apart from the fact they were a pair of psychos!'**

Belle and Sam were thrown into prison at one point for horse-stealing. After they got out, Sam disappeared and Belle got a new bloke called Middleton. Everyone thought he had got rid of Sam, but Middleton was found full of bullets and Sam reappeared. Belle didn't seem too bothered either way. One revolting, personality-disordered criminal is much the same as the next.

By this time Belle and Sam were appearing on government posters with a $10,000 reward. (Almost tempting to arrest themselves, I would have thought.) They were eventually arrested but got off for lack of evidence. This is a euphemism for one of their mates threatening to shoot the judge.

At Christmas, Sam went into town, got pissed, argued with the local sheriff and was shot dead. So much for good will to all men. Belle mourned for about twelve minutes and got another lover in. Flavour of the month was another Native American, Jim July. Belle persuaded him to turn himself in, because she thought there was too little evidence to convict him. She also promised to support him. They set off to their local fort and stopped off at a B and B. The next day Jim went on alone and

*Sitting on a horse sideways was a piece of piss until the bastard started to move*

Belle rode back. Riding alone along the trail, she was shot out of the saddle by an unknown gunman. The identity of the killer was never established. It could have been Jim, or it could have been Belle's son with whom she had an incestuous relationship. Or it could just have been someone in the vicinity because in the Wild West everyone was such a crap shot they could have hit anyone.

# bonnie parker

was a tiny little dainty thing. She was born in 1911 into a family of devout Baptists. Her father was a bricklayer who died when Bonnie was four, so at least the family didn't have to put up with him talking about building technology. Bonnie's mother took her to live in Cement City near Dallas, which just goes to show what wild imaginations American town planners have.

At the age of sixteen Bonnie married her childhood sweetheart, Roy Thornton, who disappeared soon after the marriage to serve a prison sentence for ninety-nine years. Bonnie obviously decided she couldn't wait for another seeing-to until she was a hundred and fifteen and when she was working as a waitress, she met Clyde Barrow. He had been in and out of trouble since he was a kid. (I think Trouble is a small town near Chicago.)

## 'Bonnie obviously decided she couldn't wait for another seeing – to until she was a hundred and fifteen'

Clyde had spent time as a child in a boys' reformatory which hadn't done the trick, since he had been a petty criminal all his life. Before the pair could get to know each other properly, Clyde was sentenced to two years in prison. Bonnie decided she couldn't wait this long and smuggled a gun in to him.

(Must have been a hell of a cake.) He broke out, but only for four days, because he rather stupidly got caught after an armed robbery.

This time he was given fourteen years. Poor old Bonnie must have thought she was destined to become a nun. However, Clyde was released from prison when Texas elected a woman governor. Bet she's kicking herself now. Clyde, meanwhile, was probably having a bit of trouble kicking himself, because while he was in prison, he'd lost two toes. Not, as you might think, in a mailbag sewing accident – he got a mate to chop them off with an axe so he could avoid hard labour. I would have tried 'I've got a tummy ache' first.

*Photographers were a bit scared of Bonnie who was known to have shot them if they didn't catch her good side. Problem was, he didn't have a good ide*

Bonnie and Clyde decided to start a criminal gang. This, obviously, wasn't the sort of career your parents would be very impressed with, so Bonnie told her mum she was going to do a job demonstrating cosmetics. I think my mum would have preferred me to be a gangster.

The lovers formed the Barrow Gang (had to be his name didn't it?) and within a few months, Bonnie and Clyde had already shot dead three people. Their main targets were small-town banks, cafes and petrol stations. Not exactly aiming high, were they? I wonder if they would have been quite so dangerous individually. Some couples are a lethal combination. Look at Richard and Judy. At first, Bonnie and Clyde had a good time, staying in posh hotels and buying expensive clothes. The Press loved

# a load of old ball crunchers

them and nicknamed them 'Suicide Sal' and 'the Texas Rattlesnake'. I think I'd have gone for Batty Bonnie and the Toeless Toerag.

All this press attention meant that Bonnie and Clyde were recognised everywhere, so they couldn't stay in hotels any more. They were forced to sleep in cars and exist on peanut butter sandwiches and ice cream. Sounding a bit more attractive isn't it?

Bonnie and Clyde were joined by a third friend in crime, William Jones. He is supposed to have had an affair with Bonnie, who by all accounts was a bit of a nymphomaniac. Still, considering men think women are nymphomaniacs if they have more than one bloke, I think we can dismiss that.

Clyde's brother, Buck, and his wife, Blanche, had joined Bonnie and Clyde by now. They rented an apartment in Missouri in a respectable neighbourhood, which turned out to be a mistake. These neighbours didn't miss a trick and one of them phoned the police and reported he had seen a great deal of suspicious coming and going at their place. Hurrah for Neighbourhood Watch, or if you live in Hampstead, Neighbourhood Swatch.

The police sent two squad cars to Bonnie and Clyde's apartment on a routine investigation. This turned into a shoot-out which left two policemen dead. I suppose it didn't occur to Bonnie and Clyde that their chances of having to do a very good impression of a colander in the near future were rising with every poor bugger they shot.

Now Bonnie and Clyde couldn't even rent a flat. They were forced to sleep in the car and anyone who has ever tried to have a decent night's kip in a car and woken up dribbling with an ashtray in their hair will know this doesn't leave you in the best of moods.

Bonnie realised it wouldn't be long before she and Clyde moved in to that big nosey neighbourhood in the sky, and decided she wanted to see her mum. A secret rendezvous was arranged, but when her mum asked Bonnie whether she could get her any free lipstick samples, Bonnie suspected that she hadn't been reading the papers.

Clyde tried to check them into hell early when he ignored a sign on the road saying a bridge over a gorge had collapsed and they drove into midair. (Bear in mind the

*ike many gangsters, Bonnie only*
*hot her own kind – people with*
*bysmal dress sense*

importance of signs like this if you're about to take your driving test.) Bonnie was trapped in the wreckage and the car caught fire. A farmer and his mate pulled her clear and got a bit suspicious when the charred sack that was Bonnie insisted she didn't need a doctor. Farmer Giles called the police so Clyde nicked his car. Good job he wasn't driving a tractor. . . Clyde and gang checked into a holiday cabin, Clyde telling everyone that Bonnie had been injured in an oilstove explosion while camping. Perhaps the other holiday-makers might have been more convinced if he said she'd forgotten to put on her Factor Twenty. Fellow holiday-makers became suspicious when the Barrow Gang kept their curtains drawn all the time. Oh come on, we've all had holidays that boring.

The gang's holiday got a lot less boring when they had another shoot-out with the police in which Buck was shot in the head and Blanche temporarily blinded by glass. Not dissimilar to a fortnight in Florida then. Bonnie was still in agony from her burns, so I don't suppose hiding out in the woods was her first choice of venue. To make themselves feel better, Bonnie sent William Jones out to get five chicken dinners and, wouldn't you just know it, he was followed back by the police. Perhaps one of the chickens got suspicious. The obligatory shoot-out followed and Buck and Blanche were captured.

# 'Bonnie and Clyde decided to start a criminal gang. This, wasn't the sort of career your parents would be very impressed with'

Bonnie and Clyde escaped back to Texas, Clyde disguised as a woman in a blonde wig. They organised a prison breakout for a bloke called Ray Hamilton, shooting a few more people on the way. Eventually the rozzers got a tip-off from one of Clyde's friends. Six officers waited in bushes at the side of the road. As the couple's car drew up, they could see Bonnie eating a sandwich and laughing. They peppered the car with bullets. Well, it might have improved the sandwich.

# elizabeth bathory

is about as Gothic as you can get. She is thought to be one of the sources of inspiration for Bram Stoker's legend of Dracula, the other being Dame Shirley Porter.

Elizabeth Bathory was Hungarian by birth and popped into the world in 1561. She lived in the Carpathian Mountains, which looked like a Hammer Horror film set with brooding castles, dense forests and peasants with big warts on their noses. As a girl, Elizabeth was beautiful with long fair hair and a lovely complexion. She was therefore top marriage fodder and was married off to an aristocratic soldier at the age of fifteen and became mistress of a castle. This wasn't that different from being mistress of a normal house except there were a lot more stairs, rats and loads of really irritating screaming coming from the dungeons.

Elizabeth's husband was away on military campaigns quite a lot and she got very bored. There was no *This Morning* with Richard and Judy or *Hello* to keep her spirits up, so she got in a gang of mates. Now these weren't

**Gas Mark Three for Keith Floyd's boiled virgin's heads was a bit difficult to achieve on an open fire**

your common or garden jumble sale organisers and coffee morning chatterers, but a bunch of witches, sorcerers and alchemists who taught her the black arts. The black arts of course consist of skills such as how to turn your mum into a frog, how to turn your husband into a mouse and how to magic up the book *Frog And Mouse Recipes For Beginners*.

Elizabeth's equipment consisted of special flesh-tearing silver pincers and a manual of tortures her husband had used when fighting the Turks. The woman wasn't bored, she was a borderline psychopath. Elizabeth also displayed a taste for flagellation, which she had learned from her aunt. Cor blimey wot a family. I suppose the uncle strangled cats for a hobby.

Elizabeth's husband died when she was in her forties. She wanted a replacement, but realised she was a bit too wrinkled and ugly to stand much of a chance at Hungarian Dateline. She had spent her life until that point overindulging and looked older than she was. This happens to so many women who then get themselves on the treadmill of the search for eternal youth. HRT is always an option, but I can't think of anything worse than being gagging for it when I'm seventy and fighting the three hundred other old ladies in the home for the one old git left alive. Elizabeth was determined to find a way of regaining her youth. One day, she slapped the

*'See what happens when you let fat birds into Stringfellows?'*

face of a servant girl and her nails drew blood. She was convinced that the part of her where the blood had landed was much fresher and younger than before. I don't know which bit the blood landed on. Before she went any further she should have tried it out on someone's testicles. Making those smooth would have been the acid test.

Elizabeth's alchemists convinced her that the blood was the answer to more youthful looks and she became obsessed with the idea that bathing in and drinking the blood of young virgins would make her more gorgeous. It may sound ridiculous, but I'm sure that most women don't know what liposomes are and they continue to smear them on like there's no tomorrow.

## 'The black arts of course consist of skills such as how to turn your mum into a frog, how to turn your husband into a mouse and how to magic up the book Frog And Mouse Recipes For Beginners'

The problem now for Elizabeth was to get hold of some virgin's blood. The Body Shop wasn't doing it and it wasn't something you could sling together from a few leftovers in the cupboard. So, in the middle of the night, with her gang, Elizabeth would roam round the countryside looking for young girls. (Although it's odds-on that any

# a load of old ball crunchers

*'Do I look like a virgin you silly cow?' was a question often asked of Elizabeth Bathory*

young girls wandering round the countryside at night probably weren't virgins.) The 'virgins' would be taken back to the castle, hung in chains and their blood used for the Countess's bath, the finest being saved for her to drink. (A Bloody Elizabeth being a slight variation on A Bloody Mary.) Elizabeth carried on in this vein (sorry) for five years, which is how long it took for her to realise her plan wasn't really working. She thought this might well be down to the coarseness of the girls she was using, and decided to step up the social ladder, opening an academy to teach young girls social graces. She was helped in this enterprise by a woman called Dorotta Szentes, known as Dorka. Between them, they treated the pupils with inhuman cruelty. This hadn't mattered too much when it was just a load of plebby peasant girls but then Elizabeth and Dorka got careless and the bodies of four girls were found by villagers after they had been thrown over the castle walls. That deportment business with the books on your head is a bugger to get right isn't it?

# 'I can't think of anything worse than being gagging for it when I'm seventy and fighting the three hundred other old ladies in the home for the one old git left alive'

The villagers took the bodies of the girls away and identified them, so at last old wrinkle-bottom was sussed. The Emperor of Hungary ordered that the Countess be brought to trial. However, because she was an aristocrat she could not be arrested. Bloody typical. But surprisingly, Parliament passed a new act so that she would not be able to slip through their hands. At the hearing in 1610 it was said that Elizabeth had murdered six hundred girls. Dorka and her witches were burnt at the stake, which didn't do much for their youthful looks. Elizabeth escaped execution because she was posh, but she was walled up in a tiny room of her castle and kept alive with scraps of food. She died four years later.

# lady caroline lamb <small>was a right</small>

one. She suffered from one of the worst cases of unrequited love in history. Most women have been in this condition at one time or another, but they tend to give up quite quickly after they've tortured themselves with a bit of poetry and some Leonard Cohen. Cazza went for it big style.

## 'Cazza was dainty and delicate with blonde curly hair, a bit like David Gower. She had a volatile nature and got nervous and over-excited at times, a bit like Gazza'

Cazza was the daughter of Lord and Lady Bessborough and was dainty and delicate with blonde curly hair, a bit like David Gower. She had a volatile nature and got nervous and over-excited at times, a bit like Gazza. She was married to William Lamb, the son of Lord Melbourne, who was very rich and staid, a bit like Nigel Mansell. Cazza tried to be a good wife, but she and her husband were just not compatible. They had a son together who was very whiny and sickly and had to be looked after by a nurse because Cazza couldn't cope.

The Lambs lived out in Hertfordshire, where Cazza had nothing to do except reading and writing letters. She had too much nervous energy whereas her husband was completely lethargic. Cazza flirted with other men to try and get him going, but he didn't even notice. Her mother-in-law heard she was hanging around with no-good boyos and getting presents and wrote to say her behaviour was 'disgusting'. But that's the job of a mother-in-law.

*zza prepares to fire a plate of
apes at Byron's mush*

When she was nearly thirty Cazza met Byron, the poet. She had read his poem 'Childe Harold' and said that she had to meet him. I suppose it's a bit like Paula Yates listening to an INXS single and thinking she must have that Michael geezer. Caroline was told that Byron had a club foot and bit his nails. To this she replied, 'If he is as ugly as Aesop, I must see him'. Perhaps you didn't know Aesop was ugly. Oh yes indeed, his ugliness is fabled.

Cazza and Byron first set eyes on each other at Lady Jersey's ball. Byron had quite an impact on Cazza who was so overcome by his gorgeousness she had to turn away and go home. In her diary that day, she wrote, 'He is mad, bad and dangerous to know'. Perfect material for a completely pointless affair which would drive her mad, then.

When Cazza was out riding one day, she called on Lord and Lady Holland, who told her they were expecting Byron. Cazza panicked, because like most women she hadn't spent fourteen hours in front of the dressing table putting her make-up on. She had to make do with running upstairs to the bathroom to do a quick repair job. When she came down, Byron looked her up and down and was immediately interested. The fact is men couldn't give a toss if your hair is combed and your lippy on straight. Signs of life are normally enough for a lot of them. Notice that Byron didn't panic and get a new foot and some false nails.

# 'Cazza kept the wild side of her personality in check because she knew Byron liked quiet women. Byron did bog all to make any changes for her, because he was a bloke'

Byron asked permission to call on Cazza, which is code for nomping her stupid for the next few months. From that point on Byron and Cazza were inseparable. They were asked to parties as if they were man and wife, which meant they were always late, bickered as they arrived and flirted with lots of other people I suppose.

Cazza kept the wild side of her personality in check because she knew Byron liked quiet women. Byron did bog all to make any changes for her, because he was a bloke. Cazza wrote loads and loads of adoring letters to Byron and it wasn't long before she was really getting on his nerves. He tried to move away from her but she made sure she went to all the parties he was going to and that she ended up in his carriage. Byron always ended up in her vagina. If Cazza was not actually invited to a party Byron was at, she would wait outside in the street for him. Lots of blokes find it very hard to cope with women that are madly in love with them. They prefer the woman to play games with them . . . like football.

Cazza watched Byron endlessly and even got someone to spy on him. She also disguised herself as a tradesman and went to his lodgings, where she managed to get past his valet and throw herself at his feet. I'm surprised a closer look at the clubbed one didn't even put her off a teensy bit.

Byron was getting really irritated by now. Cazza ran away and Byron went and got her back. She said that if he left London, she would do it again. At this point the poor old husband (remember him?) came back on the scene and took Cazza off to Ireland. She continued to write to Byron and at the height of her obsession, she sent him a letter containing her pubic hair which she had ripped out. Wonder what it said on the packet, if it was a recorded delivery.

Byron kept his whereabouts secret. He was probably worried about what was going to plop on to his mat next. Plop, possibly.

When Cazza did not hear from Byron for weeks she threatened to cut her throat. She could have sent that to Byron. Luckily her mother grabbed the blade. Cazza was also seen brandishing a knife at a ball, although it's not clear whether it was for one of Byron's goolies. Byron wearily agreed to see her one more time before he left England for good, after which Cazza's husband decided to stay with her for a bit. She could have faded into obscurity, but wrote a novel, *Glenarvon*, all about Byron and various society types instead. Cazza never really recovered from Byronitis. Her first trip out after being ill didn't help, as she bumped into Byron's funeral cortège. Life's a bitch ain't it?

**'Cazza never really recovered from Byronitis. Her first trip out after being ill didn't help, as she bumped into Byron's funeral cortège'**

# sharon stone

Everyone knows Sharon Stone. She's the one in that film who crossed her legs and flashed a bit of her Aunty Mary. No pants. . . big deal. When I go on holiday, I always run out of pants after the first two days. However the 'No Knicks' syndrome has been very important for our Sharon. It does seem as though it has been the crux on which Sharon's future career depended. (Or should that be crutch? Or crotch?)

*'Just shut the fuck up about my ...ubes and take the picture asshole'*

Sharon Stone was born in Pennsylvania, which is on the American side of the Great Lakes, in March 1958. She was the second of four children and stood out from the other kids at school because she had a very high IQ and felt a freak when she was young. No one likes a mouthy kid, so she became a loner with a hatred of authority. She should have been a Wimbledon footballer.

Sharon retreated into a world of her own. Her parents were worried about her future, at least as far as jobs were concerned. Her dad kept telling her, 'There's great opportunities in engineering'. A building site may not have been the best place for Sharon to consider revealing her pubes, though, so thankfully she decided against it.

Sharon went through a period of tearing her clothes off and streaking through the house. I tried this as a teenager, but my parents went to court and got an injunction out against me to stop it on the grounds that it was putting everyone off their dinner.

Sharon's first big romance ended in tragedy as her boyfriend, Craig Grindell, who was from a very rich family, was killed whilst racing his car down a country road. Sharon was devastated and things didn't get any better as another of her boyfriends, Ray, was killed when his motorbike went out of control. One might imagine that after that, men would not be too keen to date her because she seemed to be a bit jinxed. Flashing your aunt to get another bloke seems a little extreme however.

# 'So Sharon decided to move to Hollywood despite the fact that with her name she could easily have moved to Basildon and lived out her life as a fantasy Essex girl'

In 1976, Sharon was accepted by the Eileen Ford Model Agency in New York. This was the chance she had been waiting for. She left straight away for The Big Apple, with the added advantage that the men there would not know her dating history. However, she found the strict dieting associated with being a model very difficult. She lived with an agent from the Eileen Ford Agency and was forbidden to bring soda into the flat. Not soda you use to pour down the lav, but fizzy drinks. She was only allowed to have crackers and water. Yum! It's a model's life for me. . . not.

After that, Sharon spent some time in Italy, but wasn't keen on the men. I can't blame her. They do seem to slaver over women more than your average European, which may explain why the streets of Rome are paved with gob. So Sharon decided to move to Hollywood and try her hand at acting, despite the fact that with her name she could easily have moved to Basildon and lived out her life as a fantasy Essex girl. Lots of jokes about Essex girls do seem to involve them whipping out their parts at the first opportunity – as though that was somehow a bad thing to do. . .

Sharon landed a part in the film *Stardust Memories*. She was personally picked out from a huge group of hopefuls by the great man Woody Allen himself. Sharon and Woody had a conversation about infinity, probably because that's how far Mr Allen's ego extends. Despite the fact that he is an intelligent, witty, intellectual

*Sharon with her environmentally-friendly plastic surgeon, who has injected her breasts with baby bio instead of silicon*

type, don't forget that Woody Allen is just another man with a penis who is always looking for somewhere new to park it.

Sharon also studied method acting. This is a form of acting where you actually take on the personality of the person you are playing in your life. Thankfully, Anthony Hopkins didn't do this for *Silence of the Lambs* or a few attractive women with big knockers would have disappeared under a parsley garnish.

# 'Flashing your aunt to get another bloke seems a little extreme however'

Sharon found being blonde in Hollywood was a problem because you tended not to be taken seriously. (Shaz, old girl, showing your vag doesn't help either.) There then followed Sharon's crap telly period of her career. You can trace most big stars back through this time in their lives. It's always such a joy to watch

something like *Bonanza* and spot someone like Sir Laurence Olivier dressed up as a barmaid spitting on the floor. During this time, Sharon met her husband to be, Michael Greenburgh. They were married in Pennsylvania in 1984, and since Michael survived unhurt, he obviously broke Sharon's jinx.

Sharon then starred in a major film, *King Solomon's Mines*. Perhaps she read it wrong and thought it said *King Solomon's Minge*. The film was a disaster and so was Sharon's marriage. She split with Michael and got a part in *Police Academy Four*. Police Academy . . . somewhat of a contradiction

***Sharon ensures that a quick peek at her Aunt Mary will be difficult by employing a load of old sheets***

in terms. The *Police Academy* series is one long knob, bum and knockers joke. Sharon got a lot of exposure doing this film, with more exposure to come.

Surely the highlight of Sharon Stone's career so far has been *War and Remembrance* with the lovely Jane Seymour, a woman who has not slapped out her equipment for public consumption – but I wish she had. Too clean, too sweet, too dull, like a nun's favourite reading.

Sharon stepped up a notch with *Total Recall*. She said Arnie Shwarzenegger taught her a lot. Must have been something other than acting then. Sharon Stone was now ready for the big flash. A split second of film launched her star into orbit and threw her into such demanding film roles as *Sliver*, where she had to masturbate in the bath. In other words, if you put clips of her films together you could almost have a film called *Big Busty Nurses* to be todged over by many a raincoat.

Sharon is now worth a packet as a film star. For someone with such a high IQ, it's a big pity that her rise to fame has been entirely dependent on showing her bits. Pants away girls and forget the exams.

# sylvia plath

was the first child of Otto and Aurelia Plath and was born in 1932 in Boston Massachusetts. She probably never set foot in Cheers though because she was not a happy person and I don't think there was a bar in Boston called Misery.

Otto died when Sylvia was eight and Slyvia became heavily dependent on her mother. Sylvia was excellent at school.

**Sylvia tries to look pleased with the cardy her granny has sent her but doesn't manage it**

Unfortunately she was tall and gangly and most of the boys were afraid of her. I'd have preferred that to most of them shouting abuse or gobbing in my shoes. Sylvia was rather shy and withdrawn and, as a teenager, tried to create a new personality for herself by using the nickname 'Sherry'. Unfortunately, this is quite a difficult thing to do, because however much you take on the personality of a witty, outgoing, fashionably dressed, omniscient socialite, you are still a schoolgirl in white socks with a big blob of custard on your cardy.

Sylvia's first writing was published in the *Boston Globe* and the *Christian Science Monitor*. She was young, so I suppose we can forgive her for the *Christian Science Monitor*. Christian Science is a religion which makes millions out of people's low self-esteem and turns Americans into zombies. Why bother? Most of them are watching enough crap telly to do it all on their own.

At college, Sylvia had quite a social life and records in her diary the number of dates she was asked on and some of the reasons she gave for turning them down, including saying she had TB or cancer. I suppose she couldn't say she was washing her hair like the rest of us, because she wouldn't have qualified as a poet. Come to think of it, has any woman ever said she is washing her hair? It's not like it takes all night is it? I'd just say, 'I don't want to go out with you because I've heard you've got a very small todger'.

## 'I'd just say, "I don't want to go out with you because I've heard you've got a very small todger"'

Sylvia's diary reveals that she had a very nihilistic view of the world, which was later to manifest itself as depression. I feel that the people that don't have a nihilistic view of the world are the ones with the problem. It's so screamingly obvious to most of us that the power in the world is in the hands of a bunch of nasty, thicko arseholes, that anyone who's cheerful about that must either be mad or a nasty, thicko arsehole.

## 'I feel that the people that don't have a nihilistic view of the world are the ones with the problem'

# a load of old ball crunchers

*'Hi! I'm Sherry and I go for it big time, buddy!'*
*'. . . Oh, all right then, I'm Sylvia and you can't date me cause I've got Necrolysing Fascititis'*

In the summer of 1952, while she was working as a waitress, Sylvia won a $500 fiction prize from *Mademoiselle* magazine. (Mmm, that sounds radical and feminist doesn't it?) It was at this point that Sylvia decided to become a writer. She was also becoming more obsessed with the troubles of the world, of which there were plenty at the time; Korea, the McCarthy witch-hunts and, of course, those horrible pointy bras that women had to wear. By the end of 1952, Sylvia was working very hard and suffered from insomnia and inexplicable anger. Also, her periods stopped for about five months, so the inexplicable anger couldn't have been PMT. This amenorrhoea (good word) would have cheered me up considerably, because much as I try, I cannot be one of those women who gets a dog to pull me along on a skateboard while I screech with delight. Twelve carthorses maybe.

Sylvia accepted a job for the summer on *Mademoiselle* magazine. She found it tough and hit a low point, attempting suicide twice. She was given ECT treatment and seems to have got a bit better. Most people think ECT is a treatment given without anaesthetic, as a punishment, because it was like that in *One Flew Over The Cuckoo's Nest*. Well, it isn't. Although I'm sure there are hundreds of women in Hollywood who would like to put fifteen thousand volts through Jack Nicholson's testicles.

After graduation, Sylvia was awarded a Fellowship at Newnham College Cambridge. At the time, there were ten men at Cambridge to every one woman, which I reckon is about what women are worth. Sylvia noticed and admired a young poet called Ted Hughes. Their first encounter involved a very ferocious kiss which left Ted's face bleeding. Of course it's possible Sylvia had missed dinner.

Sylvia became besotted with Ted and eventually they married and had a honeymoon in Spain. On their return, they lived for a while with Ted's family in Brontë country and planned to move to London, that metropolis of cheery fulfilled people, give or take a few hundred thousand depressed and lonely old bastards. Sylvia was very happy at first and wrote *The Colossus and Other Stories*. In 1960, she became pregnant, which she found difficult, because she was pushed into the background while Ted's fame grew. This is a perennial problem for pregnant women, stuck at home with a massive tum, while the other half swans about, tum empty, having a great time.

Sylvia began to get jealous of things Ted did and made her feelings known in no uncertain terms by shouting, screaming and destroying Ted's work. Difficult for some women to do if you're married to a lazy old bugger that doesn't do any.

Sylvia and Ted moved to Devon and things began to fall apart. They had two children and Sylvia suffered badly from post-natal depression which was not acknowledged for a long time, mainly because women's feelings weren't felt to be that important. (Not like it is now.) At one point, Sylvia intercepted a mysterious call for Ted (from the 'other woman'). She reacted very badly and burned Ted's manuscripts. By this time, their marriage was in serious trouble. Ted called Sylvia 'a hag'. Not the most poetic or respectful of responses. Ted moved out and Sylvia decided to move back up to London. Sylvia found a flat in Primrose Hill but her mental state was precarious by this point and she committed suicide. Poor old Sylvia, but at least people don't say 'Who is she?', about her any more.

# flora macdonald

was born in the Outer Hebrides in 1722. Her father was called Ranald Macdonald. Had he only changed a couple of letters of his name, things could have been so different. Perhaps if he hadn't named his daughter after a brand of margarine as well, she might have faded into obscurity.

*Flora often got mistaken for a small cottage garden*

Flora's dad was an important man who held land; in fact he was next down from a clan chief. Flora's mum, 'I Can't Believe It's Not Butter', was the daughter of a Presbyterian minister and when Flora's dad died a year after her birth, there were two farms to look after. Unfortunately, on the island, the food was a bit crap. (That's not like McDonalds of course.) There wasn't much meat or any dairy produce so most people lived on a diet of oatmeal, fish and broth which was made by boiling limpets with milk. What a horrible McSoup that sounds.

In 1745, things weren't going well for Flora. South Uist was a place of misery and suffering and bad weather for years had turned the fields into quagmires. Crops were expected to be poor, so Flora was having to spread herself very thin. (Geddit?) However, a rumour spreading through the Highlands that the Jacobites were coming cheered people up a bit. Bonnie Prince Charlie carried the hopes of the Jacobites that a Catholic would be restored to the throne of England. If you want to know more about him, look in *A Load Of Old Balls*. He had arrived in Scotland on 21 July 1745, but despite initial successes, it all went horribly wrong at Culloden and Charlie was forced to flee. He was smuggled off the mainland and out to the isles and eventually ended up on South Uist, where of course he met Flora.

# 'They decided to make him a special costume as none of their clothes were big enough for him. So, he wasn't Bony Prince Charlie then'

Hanoverian forces discovered he was on the island and surrounded it, so it was time for Charlie to move on again. Flora had a very clever idea to disguise Charlie as a woman. They decided to make him a special costume as none of their clothes were big enough for him. So, he wasn't Bony Prince Charlie then.

They made him a quilted petticoat and a dress made out of calico with sprigs of lilac flowers on it. Had he been spotted wandering round the town, I think it's highly likely he might have been employed as a model for Laura Ashley. This outfit was finished off with a dun-coloured cloak, an apron, a cap, stockings and French garters. Done up like a big dog's breakfast, Charlie and his supporters settled down for a bit of a feast. Half-way through, word arrived that General

Campbell had landed and now they were really in the soup. Everyone panicked and legged it.

A letter had been sent on to Skye describing Charlie as 'Betty Burke', an Irish girl who was a spinster in the true sense of word, as opposed to an unattached leper with only pain and misery to look forward to. Charlie's friend, Felix, was not allowed to go with them, possibly because he was a tin of cat food. Charlie had a big Betty Showbizz tantrum.

*Flora is introduced to the leader of Spandau Ballet, who has half-heartedly adopted a 'grunge' look*

He also wanted to have a pistol under his petticoat, but Flora wouldn't allow it, because if it was discovered it would give him away. Charlie pointed out that if they looked that closely, they might notice other equipment under his petticoat which would be likely to give him away. Charlie was allowed to keep his crab stick, a short cudgel, not a snack he'd just purchased from the fishmongers. The gang then set sail over the sea to Skye and I for one wish they hadn't because we might have been spared the Des O'Connor and Roger Whittaker rendition of that ditty.

# a load of old ball crunchers

Charlie finally escaped to France, but Flora was suspected of helping him and arrested and imprisoned on HMS Furnace, where she was interrogated. She kept her composure and tried not to drop too many people in the shit, difficult on a boat where the sanitary conditions mirrored the conditions in the men's lavs in pubs down the Old Kent Road. Flora was transferred to a couple more ships moored off Leith in Edinburgh and given quite a few privileges. She became a bit of a celebrity and received many visitors, but only those who could stand the smell, obviously. A writer at the time describing conditions on some of the prison ships talks of an 'odious distemper peculiar to Scotsmen'. Unwashed sporrans maybe.

# 'The first two years of their marriage were very happy. Well, it takes about two years to discover someone's worst habits'

Flora was eventually taken to London and kept at a house for low risk prisoners. She wasn't there long, because a general amnesty was declared and she returned to Scotland in search of a husband. Not for her the life of Betty Burke, spinster.

Here she met and married Alan Macdonald, very handy as he had the same name and was a bit of a looker. The first two years of their marriage were very happy. Well, it takes about two years to discover someone's worst habits, as they tend to keep such delights as cleaning out their ears with your best cutlery to themselves in the first flush of romance.

Flora had four sons and one daughter before things started to go wrong. There was cattle plague (which of course we've managed to sort out easily these days) and crop failure. Many islanders saw emigration as their only means of economic salvation. The Macdonalds set sail for North Carolina in 1774. These voyages were hardly *QE2* standard and half the people on them died before they reached their destination, so it was more like an 18/30 holiday.

The family settled on a plantation of seventy acres and Flora had to work very hard. At that time the War of Independence was getting into full swing and Alan Macdonald, who was loyal to the British Government, recruited an army. His highland regiment suffered a terrible defeat at Moores Creek, and Alan was taken prisoner and marched a hundred and fifty miles north. Flora's worry over Alan led to ill-health, although at least she didn't have to go for a hundred and fifty mile ramble. Carolina was a bit of a dangerous place as places are when there are rampant soldiers on the loose and Flora suffered insults and robbery. They might as well have stayed in Scotland and moved to the Gorbals.

Alan was finally released and they headed for Nova Scotia. Flora decided to return to Britain while Alan stayed out there, returning to Skye after eleven years. He had only spent three of those years with Flora, which may explain why their marriage lasted.

Flora died in 1790, but her legend lived on in lots of sandwiches.

# lilith

**lilith** is a mythical figure in Judaism who sounds great. She is portrayed as a female demon who seduces men. What a great job eh? Obviously, Lilith's job was too popular with women and far too many applied, so they were brought down to earth by finding out she was also a child-killer: not quite such an attractive prospect, apart from the odd occasion on which I would like to murder a few of the little buggers round where I live who have had my car radio about seven times.

## 'Lilith pointed out that God had made her and Adam equal and so she didn't see why she should lie underneath Adam'

Lilith is also supposed to have been Adam's first wife, created from dust to be her husband's equal. This is rather refreshing to hear considering that most women at the time were certainly not on a par with men, although Lot's wife was in great demand when the first chippy opened.

In her role as a demon, Lilith becomes active at night. She seizes men and forces them to copulate with her. I'm not bad at the seizing bit, I just can't seem to get the forcing to copulate bit right. There is actually only one reference to Lilith in the Hebrew scriptures, in Isaiah, which remarks that Lilith shall be at rest amongst the wild animals in the desert, although how she could get any kip with the Millwall supporters club singing and vomiting everywhere, I do not know. Lilith's character is paid more attention in post-biblical Jewish literature. In the Babylonian Talmud, Lilith is portrayed as having a woman's face, long hair and wings. (I don't blame her, Tampax just don't do the job like Always Ultra do.) Also men are warned against

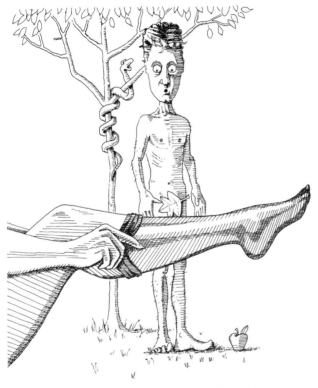

sleeping alone in case they are seized by Lilith. Funnily enough I've never heard that excuse when someone's chatted me up.

In early commentary on the Bible, Lilith is referred to as a child-killer who kills her own children when no others are available. So unavoidably we have the seduction of men linked to infanticide. No wonder women had to take care if they were planning a night of seducing someone, it seems as though suddenly they might find themselves accused of bumping off their own kids. They could just have had a female baddie who nomped everyone in sight and raided sweet shops. She would have had a huge following in every sense of the word.

Should Lilith enter your house and try and smother your baby, there is a way of catching her. Apparently you can trap her in an overturned bowl. What you do with her then isn't clear, but I suppose you could try some milk and sugar. A biblical commentary called *The Alphabet of Bensira* relates that when God created Adam he thought it was not a good idea for men to live alone. So perhaps God is a bloke after all, who thinks that men should live with someone who will pick up their clothes after them, cook their dinner, iron their shirts and tape *Match of the Day* for them, the ultimate sacrifice when *Kavanagh QC* is on the other side.

## 'Lilith is portrayed as the demon queen of the underworld, a kind of cross between Tina Turner and Alice Cooper'

When Adam and Lilith were put together, they immediately quarrelled. This was because Lilith pointed out that God had made her and Adam equal and so she didn't see why she should lie underneath Adam. Fair point, but at least if sex is boring you can count the number of cracks on the ceiling, rather than sitting astride someone and looking up their nose. Following the row, Lilith cursed God's name and flew away. Adam moaned so much that God sent three angels to get her back. God had decided that if Lilith refused he would punish her by letting a hundred of her children die every day. So, God's a child-killer now as well is he?

The angels found Lilith at the Red Sea, but she refused to return. When she was told of God's proposed punishment, she vowed to take revenge in the form of inflicting harm on all males up to the eighth day after birth and females up to the twelfth day. All very well having a big ruck with God, but what about all the poor little babies that were going to get it because they couldn't agree.

## 'She is the owner of all the seed that every man has wasted in his lifetime and let's face it, that's going to be a fair bit isn't it?'

In medieval mystical works, Lilith is portrayed as the demon queen of the underworld, a kind of cross between Tina Turner and Alice Cooper. Lilith is supposed to have been one of two harlots who stood in judgement over Solomon. He also suggested a child should be cut in half. The biblical Social Services would have had a field day.

The other thing that Lilith does is collect men's sperm, not such a great job really. Apparently she is always lying in wait anywhere it is spilled, like an employee from an infertility clinic who has taken the job a little bit too seriously. She is the owner of all the seed that every man has wasted in his lifetime and let's face it, that's going to be a fair bit isn't it? Because Lilith gets her hands on so much sperm, she is always giving birth to thousands of little devils; but don't worry, they are fairly harmless. They do things like turning milk and wine and snarling girls' hair. Well, now I've got a good excuse for the next time my hair looks like Bob Geldof's.

## a load of old ball crunchers

The sperm-collection business reminds me of a story a psychiatrist told me once about a sperm phobic. Her treatment was to be gradually exposed to more and more sperm, leading up to the *pièce de résistance* – a bath in the stuff. (Quite a shallow one.) The donors were a bunch of medical students, which explains why I have always thought they were wankers.

Belief in Lilith as child-killer persisted until the nineteenth century and then faded away, like the conversation of a man who wakes up after a one-night stand.

For most Jews she is now relegated to medieval superstition, although for some Jewish women, she is seen as a model of female strength and independence.

**'Belief in Lilith as child-killer persisted until the nineteeth century and then faded away, like the conversation of a man who wakes up after a one-night stand'**

# 29

# lady godiva is a legendary figure. Almost

everyone will be able to tell you what she did. However, for a huge percentage of those people, the extent of their knowledge stops there. They don't know who she was, why she was there and what happened next.

So who was Lady G? Was she someone who found the Coventry weather too hot and oppressive, a Page Three Girl looking for a bit of publicity, or someone who nipped out halfway through her bath to replace her rubber duck at Boots?

## 'Lady Godiva was less of your Linda Lusardi and more of your Sister Wendy'

Well, Godiva was the wife of Earl Leofric of Mercia. She was not happy with the amount of tax that her husband was charging the occupants of the city and begged him to reduce it. She didn't just ask him once though, she kept on and on about it until her husband got so fed up, he finally agreed to grant her request if she rode from one end of the place to the other completely naked. Now I know this is a very well known and accepted legend, but doesn't it strike you as rather an odd thing for her husband to ask for? He could have asked her to do one of a thousand more appropriate things; like cleaning his boots for a week, letting him go fishing more often, or going on top for a week, and yet he asked her to strip off and ride *au naturelle* through Coventry. Is this the sort of thing a normal bloke would do? Thinking about it . . . I suppose it is.

*Lady Godiva doing a bit of hesitating dressed in a curtain. At least she doesn't have to wear one all the time like some of us*

Now Lady Godiva was less of your Linda Lusardi and more of your Sister Wendy, so she wasn't about to relish the thought of jiggling her lungs through Coventry astride a throbbing nag. Because she was embarrassed, Lady Godiva insisted that all the people of Coventry stayed inside with their windows and doors bolted, so they wouldn't get a butchers.

Most women in those days had very long hair, so Lady G plastered her long tresses over her rude bits, crept out to her horse and, eyes downcast, made her way through the town. Thank God, they didn't have Spare Rib in those days or Lady G might have had to venture out with a Vinnie Jones haircut.

Apparently, the townsfolk respected her so much that all bar one obeyed her. Unable to resist the temptation, one individual, called Tom, unbarred his window, but before he could get an eyeful he was struck blind. This was of course your original Peeping Tom and if he was the sort of bloke who would do anything for a sight of a naked woman, he may have been struck blind because of another activity which requires a lot of dexterity in the wrist area.

I once saw a modern day Lady Godiva as I was driving home from work when I was a psychiatric nurse in South London. As I pulled up at some traffic lights, I saw a woman sail past on a bicycle with not a stitch on, wearing only some flowers in her hair. I thought maybe someone had spiked my coffee at work. This contemporary Lady Godiva's actions did not result in a reduced poll tax for the good burghers of Lambeth, but I discovered the next day that the woman in question had been admitted to the hospital where I work. Her bum must have been killing her.

> ## 'As I pulled up at some traffic lights, I saw a woman sail past on a bicycle with not a stitch on, wearing only some flowers in her hair. I thought maybe someone had spiked my coffee at work'

After she had completed her ordeal, Lady Godiva returned to her husband who did keep his word and abolish the taxes. There is of course some argument over the truth of the story and the other myth that when Lady G asked for a reduction in taxes for the whole county, she was asked to hang naked from the church tower singing 'The Birdy Song'. However, it is true that Leofric and Godiva raised Coventry from a small Anglo-Saxon village to a flourishing town. I'm

# a load of old ball crunchers

not surprised, I know blokes who would travel hundreds of miles to a city if they heard a naked woman had been trotting though the streets.

Godiva was deeply religious and renowned for her generosity towards the church, not to mention her regular appearances at The Pink Pussy Cat Club in Dudley. In 1043, Leofric and Godiva founded a great Benedictine priory in Coventry. They lavished riches upon the building, which attracted trade and made it famous. Leofric died in 1057, and Godiva is said to have survived him by ten years.

There are various differing accounts of Lady Godiva's ride. An alternative version to the one I have described says that the ride took place in front of the assembled citizens of Coventry. I don't know if they were all struck blind or not.

Other historians use the word 'naked' differently and say that if Leofric was as pious as he is supposed to have been, he may have just asked her to

parade though Coventry without all her jewels on. Feasible, but not as exciting.

There is a Godiva procession in Coventry which began in 1678. For the first hundred years, Godiva was played by a man. What a disappointment for all those pervy out-of-townies. Eventually, a woman got in on the act, although the Puritans banned it and middle-class Victorians turned it into a boring old costume pageant after one of the Godivas was so pissed she fell off the horse. I've ridden a horse when I was pissed and it's not easy to stay on. However, I did have my clothes on so I was not an early Sharon Stone.

# 'When Lady G asked for a reduction in taxes for the whole county, she was asked to hang naked from the church tower singing "The Birdy Song"'

# caroline of brunswick was

the wife of George IV. Their marriage was an arranged one and illustrates just how horribly wrong things can go for a Teutonic floozy and a rotund English big girls blouse.

*Sometimes Caroline would hold a Ryvita in her hand for weeks. Preferable to eating it I say*

When George and Caroline first met he took one look at her and said, 'Get me a glass of brandy, I'm not well'. She said, 'He's very fat and not as handsome as his portrait'. It was a *Blind Date* episode to make Cilla despair. George and Caroline both had shortcomings. She was loud and boorish and didn't know when to shut any of her orifices. George was fastidious, vain and sensitive. It was as if Wayne Sleep and Olive from *On The Buses* had been married off and forced to stay together to drive each other slowly insane.

## 'She was loud and boorish and didn't know when to shut any of her orifices'

As a child, Caroline was pretty wild and told lots of lies. By the age of sixteen she was quite pretty, but her behaviour was dreadful. Once, when her mother refused her permission to go to a ball, she screamed that she was pregnant and about to go into labour. A midwife was called and water was boiled, until Caroline owned up that it was a lie. More fool her stupid mother for walking into that one.

At twenty-six, unsurprisingly, Caroline was still unmarried. So her parents were orgasmic when the fat one from over the water expressed an interest. George had already married someone called Maria Fitzherbert with whom he was madly in love, but the marriage was unlawful. George also had massive debts and his dad the king said he would pay them off if George legally married someone posh and produced an heir. George agreed in good royal, selfish, egoistical style without a thought for anyone except himself, a royal tradition still popular today.

> 'That was the joy of being royalty. It didn't matter how many baths you'd had that year, how much spinach you'd got in your teeth or what an ageing old hag you looked, loads of blokes still wanted to give you one'

Caroline's good points were that she was kind and good natured. Well that will do nicely for me, thanks. Her bad points were that she was coarse (so fucking what?), and didn't wash. Perhaps she thought

# a load of old ball crunchers

it wasn't worth keeping clean, or better still, knowing George was fastidious, she just wanted to wind him up.

George and Caroline's wedding took place in St James's Palace after which he got drunk and spent most of the night snoring in the fireplace. Caroline left him there. Pity she didn't chuck a couple of firelighters on and grill a couple of burgers. Caroline can't have smelt that horrible, because George did actually manage to get her pregnant. She had what was described as 'a huge girl', so the baby clearly inherited George's stature and hopefully not his personality. George, of course, had wanted a boy and he was so miserable about it that he made himself ill and convinced himself he was dying. He had left everything to Mrs Fitzherbert and didn't want the child to have anything to do with Caroline at all. At least she and the baby had one thing in common . . . a pungent whiff which heralded their arrival anywhere.

George and Caroline had grown further and further apart until they agreed to separate, which was a bit hard as George kept sticking to the front of Caroline's dress because it had so much dinner down it. Caroline moved to Blackheath and thought that now she'd got rid of the old man, she'd have a bit of a wild time. She didn't really like English women so she had loads of parties to which she only invited men. That was the joy of being royalty. It didn't matter how many baths you'd had that year, how much spinach you'd got in your teeth or what an ageing old hag you looked, loads of blokes still wanted to give you one. Come on, we'd all take advantage of that.

Caroline also liked playing practical jokes on people who were irritating her. Having discovered her friend Lady Charlotte was pregnant, she insisted that she was pregnant too and borrowed the child of a labourer from Deptford. (Not something you could see Diana doing, is it?) She ended up raising the child, so it wasn't that great a joke.

Lady Charlotte for one didn't think this joke was very funny, because she immediately took revenge by giving a list of Caroline's lovers to the king and telling him that the little boy was actually Caroline's son. This went down like a side of beef at a vegan wedding. A commission was set up to investigate these accusations called the 'Delicate Investigation' and Caroline was cleared. She'd had so many drinks and so many men, however, that she returned to court looking like death warmed up.

Caroline had the sympathy of most of the people in the country because she wasn't allowed to see her daughter, maybe something Fergie might like to take note of. When her daughter was sixteen, she allowed her to have an affair, just to wind George up. You know what dads are like about their daughters becoming sexually active. When my dad found out I was sleeping with someone he went mad . . . threw a party. He couldn't believe I'd managed to get a shag.

At this point, the old king was just about to snuff it and Caroline's husband took control, which allowed him to put even more restrictions on her. He gave her just enough soap-on-a-rope to hang herself. Caroline had had just about enough of England. She buggered off abroad. She had started to wear a black wig which everyone said didn't suit her, but it made her very popular with early Cher fans. In

# a load of old ball crunchers

Milan, she met a soldier called Pergami, a good-looking bloke who had fought for Napoleon. He moved his whole family in with her, buying them all pegs for their noses.

When George III died, Caroline was met in France and asked to give up the crown for fifty thousand quid. She refused and returned to England where she was treated as a heroine, although quite a few people kept saying, 'Who's that fat, drunken old bag in the black wig with a red nose?'. Caroline was put on trial over her affair with Pergami. The trial went on for forty days, by which time everyone was bored shitless and didn't care what happened in the end – a bit like a Barbara Taylor Bradford novel. Caroline's defence counsel spoke for eight hours and because everyone was so fed up by then that they'd agree to anything she got off.

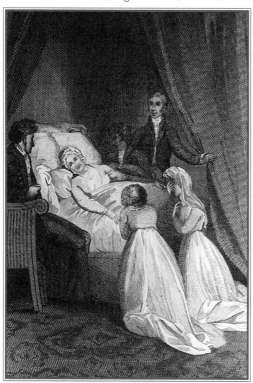

*Caroline made herself feel better by inviting lots of short women dressed in white into her bedroom*

Her husband the king was so sulky he decided he didn't want Caroline at the coronation and she was locked out of Westminster Abbey. Not long afterwards Caroline was taken ill at the Drury Lane Theatre and died from an obstruction of the bowel. Maybe she slipped and fell on a giant carton of popcorn.

# maud gonne

inspired great poetry, and any woman who inspires great poetry deserves a mention in this book. Added to that, poetry is normally written by men whose love is unrequited, so that means our heroine fought off the attentions of WB Yeats for a very long time. Anyone who has got a whinging poet harassing them at the moment might want to take a couple of leaves out of her book.

Maud's father was an army captain in Kildare. Eventually, the family settled in Dublin, the land of poetry and song. When I went to Dublin with a friend, we asked where we could listen to some Irish music. We were sent to a pub where some saddo was doing Neil Diamond covers. Some Dubliners still don't like us English.

Maud's mother died very young and so Maud was brought up by her dad. Maud was a naughty child and he found her hard to control. He can't

*n though Maud could*
*ord jewellery, she still liked*
*wear two pieces of lettuce*
*her shoulders*

have been a very good soldier, if he couldn't even manage a five-year-old girl. Maud was sent to live with her aunt in London, with the back-up of a battalion of the Royal Greenjackets. At the age of ten, she travelled round Europe, living in France, Italy and Switzerland. This meant she had no friends her own age, only older people. They must have pissed on her at Scrabble.

# a load of old ball crunchers

When she was sixteen, Maud was proposed to by a young Italian. Her father got to hear about it and brought her back to Dublin. All the poor young Italian could do was sit there and say in his pidgin (pidgin actually means Chinese jargon but I guess it's OK) English, 'Maud gone, Maud gone'.

Maud's growing awareness of the Irish problem was expanded when she watched the arrival of Lord Cavendish, the new viceroy in Dublin, and then discovered he had been murdered that night in Phoenix Park by The Invincibles – some Fenians. Nothing like choosing a name to give you confidence.

At this point, though, Maud was still a toffee-nosed rich kid who didn't give a toss about the poor. She was formally launched at a series of parties, which is what happens to debs.

It finally began to dawn on Maud that all was not well in Ireland. At a party, she heard someone discussing an Irish peasant woman who had been chucked out of her home. The speaker remarked, 'Let her die, these people must be taught a lesson. . .' – the lesson that English people are bastards, unfortunately.

Before Maud's father could resign his commission and stand for parliament supporting Home Rule, he died. Maud went to live with her uncle who told her that her father had left them hardly any money. (Not true.)

# 'Maud came of age and discovered she was loaded. This meant she could swan around for the rest of her life doing exactly what she wanted'

Maud tried to get a job as a nurse but was not accepted because she had weak lungs. In Male Fantasy Land, to get accepted as a nurse, you have to have big strong lungs. Maud then decided to become an actress, but before she could learn the 'Quality Of Mercy' speech from *The Merchant Of Venice*, her lungs exploded and she had to go to France to get better. Posh girls in those days couldn't just go down the local casualty.

# 'She had another daughter, Iseult, despite telling WB she had an aversion to sex. And the poor old bugger believed it'

# a load of old ball crunchers

While in France, Maud met Lucien Millevoye, a lawyer and journalist. He was fifteen years older than her and just separated from his wife. His big ambition was to get Alsace Lorraine back from the Germans. Millevoye persuaded Maud to give up acting and become Ireland's Joan of Arc. They became lovers. Soon after that, Maud came of age and discovered she was loaded. This meant she could swan around for the rest of her life doing exactly what she wanted.

**When Maude refused to give him one, WB wielded his pen. Judging by how thin, pale and optically-challenged he looks, that wasn't all he wielded**

At this point she met WB Yeats in London and he fell madly in love with her. This was because she was so pretty. I worry about his eyesight, though, because he failed to spot that she was five months pregnant.

Maud's child was cared for by a nurse in Paris and never impinged on her life. No wonder so many toffs are socially and emotionally handicapped. Maud got stuck into the Irish cause but lots of Irish Nationalists didn't take her work seriously and just exploited her beauty to raise funds. Same trouble I have with the Labour Party.

While Maud was stampeding round Ireland looking gorgeous, her child, Georgette, died. Maud was eaten up with guilt and began to take chloroform to sleep, which became a habit – as did WB Yeats's proposals to her. Maud managed to say 'no' to WB, but wasn't quite so successful on the drugs front. WB felt he had a spiritual marriage to Maud and she was quite happy to go along with this as he was writing much better poems than he would have done if she'd accepted him. She had another daughter, Iseult, despite telling WB she had an aversion to sex. And the poor old bugger believed it! He wasn't too happy though, when she told him all about her French lover. In fact, WB was so upset he wrote a really good poem.

## 'Whenever he said, "Come into the garden, Maud", she bogged off to Dublin'

At this point it seemed Maud held all the cards, but, as we know, life's not like that. She discovered that while she'd been gadding about, Millevoye had got fed up and got his leg over elsewhere. She and Millevoye split up. WB got really excited and saw his chance. Oh dear, not so fast. . . Time for another poem Mr Yeats.   M a u d had met someone called John McBride, who had been involved in guerilla warfare in the Boer War, which he thought might help Ireland. Maud and John did a speaking tour in America together and, lo and behold, Maud's aversion to sex managed to take a hike again. (Perhaps it was time for old WB to realise she just had an aversion to sex with him.) John asked Maud to marry him and she agreed. (WB's ditties were coming thick and fast at this point.) John and Maud married in Paris and poor old John thought Maud would settle down to a peaceful life as a bit of a housewife. But, whenever he said, 'Come into the garden, Maud', she bogged off to Dublin, where he very conveniently couldn't follow for fear of arrest.

## 'WB never gave his heart to another woman, but by this point he was fed up enough to give his part to quite a few'

# a load of old ball crunchers

John managed to come in the garden, though, and they had a son Sean. But, by now, Maud was spending a lot of time away from home, while John stayed in Paris drinking. When Maud did come home, he was violent towards her.

An article appeared in a New York newspaper entitled, 'A Brainy Woman Should Not Wed Says Maud Gonne'. John had another drink and WB wrote another poem. In the article, Maud said she reckoned that in a hundred homes you would find 75% of men quite happy and 95% of women unhappy. Not a bad assessment Maud.

*Maude forgets that unless your skirt is made of crimplene, you really have to iron it*

John finally cooked his goose when he drunkenly made a sexual assault on Maud's half-sister, Eileen, who was eighteen. Maud and John split and WB came rushing over to Paris with a couple of felt-tips in his pencil case should she turn him down again. They finally had sex but Maud wouldn't marry him. WB never gave his heart to another woman, but by this point he was fed up enough to give his part to quite a few.

Maud, meanwhile, was setting up canteens for starving schoolchildren in Ireland and doing war work in France. When the Irish Republican Brotherhood organised the Easter Uprising on 24

April 1916, John McBride joined in. The uprising lasted six days before McBride was arrested with the leaders. He was executed and Maud suddenly became quite happy to be the widow of a hero. Not something I'd find easy to do with a wife-beater.

Poor old WB asked Maud to marry him again. Maud had to think about her answer for as long as WB had to think about having a rest from writing poetry. WB took a bit of a different tack then. He proposed to Iseult, who said no, too, and then to Georgina Hyde-Lees who may have said yes, just to get rid of her silly surname.

Maud, on one of her sneaky visits to Ireland, was arrested and thrown into prison. In jail, she was allowed the concessions of a pot plant and a canary. Potential for a nice little stew there. Maud was released from prison because of bad health and tried to get away by pretending to be a nurse despite her small lungs. She went to WB's house for help and, for the first time ever, he didn't propose – in fact, he wouldn't let her in. He had finally broken the pattern. Maud was a bit pissed off. They grew apart after that. WB died first and Maud lived to a good age. Just as well, she had a lot of poems to get through.

# bette midler

was named after Bette Davis and was born in 1945 in Honolulu, Hawaii. I used to think that Honolulu was one of the most romantic places in the world, until some friends of mine went there recently and said it was quite like Croydon. This may explain why Bette wanted to escape as soon as

she could. She made a promise to herself when she grew up she would go to New York – The Big Apple. When I grew up I wanted to go to a place called The Big Roast Potato.

Bette was the only Jewish girl in a working-class, Samoan neighbourhood. She spent her childhood avoiding street fights, sitting in movie theatres and wandering the red light district. She was fascinated by 'bad girls'. So, Bette was pretty miserable as a child. She was 'a plain, fat kid' and, unfortunately, prejudice against a less than stunning appearance in women starts very early. She did have a huge chest as an adolescent but, wouldn't you

**Bette Midler on her way to watch Forrest Gump. *As you can see, she has very sensibly brought some knitting with her in case she gets bored***

just know it, the kids weren't impressed and used to tease her about it. Take heart all you plain fat kids with big knockers, your day will come!

Bette spent a year at the University of Hawaii and then got a job in a pineapple canning factory. We've all had jobs like this. I had to do fruit-picking when I was about fourteen because they wouldn't take me on at the local bakery. Grievances start young.

Bette finally made it to New York when she was twenty and lived in the Broadway Hotel for a while. She had an assortment of jobs, including typing, filing and shop work, but eventually became a dancer. She was hired by a night club to bop up and down and give the impression that something was going on. Not a good job really for someone with a massive chest.

# 'The Big Apple! When I grew up I wanted to go to a place called The Big Roast Potato'

Her first singing job was at a club in Greenwich Village, which is the sort of arty area of New York. You can tell you're in Greenwich Village if you go into a music club and Woody Allen keeps trying to get on stage and do a number with the band. Bette was always interested in torch songs, which are songs sung by fading, somewhat tired-looking female singers with titles like, 'I Saw It Through Despite The Fact That I Had A Brain Tumour' and 'None Of My Hats Would Fit Anymore'. Bette moved on and worked at The Improv which was a comedy club frequented by the likes of Richard Prior and Liza Minelli. One night, the crowd laughed at her just because of the way she looked (I know the feeling).

The experience that really shaped Bette's future and created her stage persona 'The Divine Miss M' was her sixteen-week booking at The Continental Baths. This was a sex and sauna place for gays in Manhattan. On the second night of her booking at the Baths, the

# a load of old ball crunchers

audience complained that Bette had done the same act two nights running. Just let me put something straight. Comics do not do completely different material every night. If they did they would be either geniuses or completely barking. In fact, before telly, Tony Hancock did the same stuff for sixteen years. Lazy lucky bastard.

After the complaints, Bette started to banter with the audience a bit and develop her style. My style developed from numerous lorry drivers bantering with me and calling me names. After the seven thousandth bit of abuse from some mobile beergut, I decided I was ready to go into comedy and squash a few furry dice.

Bette's musical arranger at the Baths was none other than Barry Manilow - he who writes the songs that make the whole readership of *Woman's Realm* moist. Barry, as I'm sure you're aware, followed his nose and struck off down the road on his own and stayed right in the middle of it. Meanwhile, Bette took on a manager. It shows you're hitting the big time when someone else comes along to take some of your money off you.

*'. . . Scully, it's Mulder here. I know this sounds crazy, but I think they've got the famous actress-cum-singer Bette Midler'*

Bette got booked in Las Vegas – a hideous jumble of neon in the middle of the desert, where people go to lose their shirts. By this time, Bette had three backing singers called The Harlettes and was playing Carnegie Hall. We've all heard of it, so it must be quite big.

Along with the success came another manager, Aaron Russo, who sounds like some kind of East European pudding. Everyone told Bette she should not get involved with him, but puddings are irresistible even though we know they are bad for us. They had an affair, but it was often quite difficult for Bette to sleep with him because his ego took up the whole of the bed. Aaron gave Bette lots of presents, which was very kind of him considering he bought them with her money. They were together for six years. But, as Bette's fame grew, so did Aaron's ego — and the amount of her money in his wallet.

# 'It shows you're hitting the big time when someone else comes along to take some of your money off you'

Bette Midler has always had a bit of a hard time with the critics because she is not pretty. I've yet to meet a pretty critic; but that doesn't seem to stop the mediocre, leeching, smug, self-opinionated, nasty little creeps! Sorry, did I betray a bias there?

Bette has done a number of massive tours. They really knacker you out. It's quite hard when you are hungover, shattered and Mrs PMT, to go out on stage and be cheery and together — especially if you're faced with a growling, racist crowd with a very low IQ. It's then that you realise you've got Bernard Manning's audience.

Since Bette Midler has become famous she has made numerous albums and lots of films, and all this from a plain little fat girl from Honolulu. She is quoted as saying she doesn't want to get lumped with — 'all those idle women, the women kind of women'.

# a load of old ball crunchers

I don't mind getting lumped with the idle women, it's the women kind of women I'm not keen on. Bette also says she is not very exciting offstage, so I won't bother to tell you any more about that.

# fergie

**fergie** is always described as a jolly-hockey-sticks-type-of-girl. May I just say, hockey never was, and never will be, 'jolly'. I used to get shoved in goal and I can't think of anything less pleasant than standing on an icy cold pitch, freezing your navy-blue knicks off, with a mass of vicious sticks bearing down on you. (Except perhaps a *ménage à trois* with Jeffrey Archer and Anne Widdecombe.)

Fergie was born in 1959 and was bright, but naughty. She once glued her teacher to a chair. I don't think Superglue was around in those days so the teacher probably didn't even notice because that Uhu stuff couldn't stick a Take That fan on to Robbie.

*ever having to do a day's work in her life, Fergie donated her real hands to charity, and had Mdme ussauds graft her a stick-on air for public appearances*

Fergie went to school in Hampshire, where she excelled at sport. (That's what it says on your school report if you're crap at everything else.) At her next school in Berkshire, she got six 'O' levels, all in domestic science I think.

After she left school, she did some 'cramming' (didn't we all dear), and then took a secretarial course so that she could get a job anywhere in the world. Her first job was in a London public relations firm. What do people in public relations do? All I know is that when you meet them, they don't seem to know anything about anything except polo.

## a load of old ball crunchers

Fergie helped to run a fine art publishers and her salary was £20,000 a year – less than she spends now on room service in an hour. Even in those days, before she became the Judith Chalmers of Buckingham Palace, she wangled time off for extended holidays.

Fergie's parents had split up. Her mum, Susan, ran off to South America with a polo player, Hector Barrantes, to live in his house. (Hector's House, geddit?) Polo really is the most ridiculous and pointless game in the history of the universe. A bunch of stick-wielding morons chasing something small, white and more intelligent than them, watched by a group of people with a degree in poncing off the rest of us.

## 'After she left school, she did some 'cramming' (didn't we all dear)'

Fergie has always been fond of her dad, Ron, despite his penchant for a bit of a buffing in dodgy massage parlours. He has stuck by her, too, despite her penchant for a toe-buffing from dodgy financial advisers.

Fergie had two major lovers, before Cap'n Andy. The first was Kim Smith-Bingham, not a bricklayer, unsurprisingly, but 'something in the city' – like what, a bollard? He lasted long enough to introduce her to Paddy McNally a former racing driver – judging by Nigel Mansell and Damon Hill, I bet he was the life and soul. There was a twenty-two-year age gap between Fergie and Paddy, but this didn't worry them and they became lovers. Paddy lived in Switzerland, so he was Mr Free Skiing Holiday if nothing else. They lived together for about four years, but apparently he never saw Fergie as a potential wife. (One of these gay bachelors who think the entire female population are desperate to marry them, not realising they all think he's a tosser.)

Whilst with Paddy, Fergie became friendly with Princess Diana. They met at polo – where else would a couple of carefree, knowledge-free, conscience-free, taste-free (husband-wise anyway) débutantes meet? Fergie became a frequent visitor to Buckingham Palace, where she met Andrew, lonely after having to give up Koo Stark. Andrew – a man so well liked by his Navy colleagues that, apparently, the cooks in the galley on board his ship stuck their todgers into his food before they sent it up. Yum, spotted dick.

Still, Fergie liked him and she was invited for the weekend to Windsor for a house party. Well, that's what toffs call it. Us mere mortals call it 'having friends to stay'.

***Fergie and Andrew wait for someone intelligent to tell them what to have a conversation about***

As Fergie unpacked her skis (well, you never know), she noticed from the seating plan (sent in advance so that she could work out which dress would clash best with the women nearest her) that she had been placed next to Andrew at lunch. Fergie came back from that lunch well and truly in lurve and the relationship blossomed. Their relationship was kept quiet for six months, quite an achievement for two big gobs, and, in spring, 1986, Andrew asked Fergie to marry him. She thought he was joking. I bet she wishes he had been now.

Andrew and Fergie had to wait for the Queen's permission. Surprisingly, the Queen gave it. Perhaps she got confused and thought Andrew wanted to marry the manager of Manchester United.

# a load of old ball crunchers

At her wedding, Fergie winked and pulled silly faces. This was felt to be unacceptable behaviour for a member of the Royal Family, who (because of Queen Victoria, I suppose) are all supposed to look as miserable as sin and make a very good job of it.

## 'This was felt to be unacceptable behaviour for a member of the Royal Family, who are all supposed to look as miserable as sin and make a very good job of it'

Fergie kept working for a while after her wedding, but was made redundant at the first opportunity, or perhaps I should say downsized to use the contemporary parlance. The Press wanted Fergie downsized, too, or down a size, and moaned on ad infinitum about her bum. This was about the only thing that I liked about her. Within a very short space of time, the Press had metamorphosed Fergie from 'loveable wild-child' to 'irresponsible old slapper'. She went on tours and left the children behind, she skied until her feet became curved and she put a paper bag over her head on a flight from America – something Garry Bushell wanted me to do ages ago. (I've managed to resist just to torture him.) Not only that, she wrote a children's book, the proceeds of which were supposed to go to charity (and didn't). To cap it all, she was featured in *Hello*, the magazine that makes your brain, at least, go supermodel size.

Everyone despised Fergie and Andrew's newly built mansion, too, which looked like an Asda supermarket. Fergie and Andrew's taste-score plummeted into the nine items or less category.

Fergie continued to make more blunders culminating in the now famous toe-sucking incident. This caused the Press to have a multiple orgasm and ejaculate page after page of blurry pictures into their respective rags. By now, the fairytale marriage was well and truly over. If nothing else, Fergie's story tells all of us who were read stories about girls marrying a handsome prince, that the happy-ever-after bit is bollocks.

# mary shelley

was the daughter of Mary Wollstonecraft and William Godwin. If you want to know about Mary Wollstonecraft, have a butchers elsewhere in this book.

There were five children in the Godwin household from two mothers. They were treated in a very grown-up way and were taken out to dinner and to the theatre with Godwin's friends. Children who

are given an adult role before they are old enough are immensely irritating. Anyone who has phoned a friend and had to run the gamut of their child first, will know what I mean.

Mary Godwin and Percy Shelley were heading on a collision course. Shelley, the poet, was a bit of a tearaway who had been chucked out of Oxford University for writing a pamphlet on atheism, a decision that, no matter how hard he prayed, was not reversed. After Oxford, he married sixteen-year-old Harriet Westbrook. She was sweet, open and honest, and people said you could learn everything you needed to know about her in one meeting. Percy

*Mary found it very hard to get inspiration unless she was wearing the Lord Mayor's chain*

and Harriet had a child and Perce found the responsibility hard to take. They argued constantly. Things weren't looking good for Harriet.

They looked even worse when Perce met and fell madly in love with Mary. Mary was hooked too, (as most of us would be with a wild, good-looking poet). Poor old Harriet hoped it would be a passing infatuation, but that was about as likely as Queen Victoria having a lesbian affair. Perce and Mary eloped to France. I've always thought eloping sounds romantic but this wasn't. They left London at four o'clock in the morning, it took twelve hours to get to Dover (obviously went by Eurostar), and then they had to sit in an open boat in pouring rain, throwing up everywhere for hours, until they got to Calais. Mary's sister, Jane, went with them. She must have been even more bonkers. Not even a shag in it for her.

Eventually, the trio came back, and Perce suggested to Harriet that she came to live with him and Mary. By this stage, he had conveniently decided that Harriet was just a very good friend. Harriet must have been very happy about this. She might be only a friend but she was also up the duff again with Perce's child. To complicate things, Mary was pregnant too.

To complicate things even more, at this point Jane changed her name to Claire. You'd think if she was making the effort, she'd at least have pushed the boat out with something a bit wild, like Tinkerbell or Fifi Trixibelle.

# 'There we were assuming they sat at home sewing or reading or went to church and the whole lot of them were at it like rabbits'

When Harriet's child was born, jealousy got the better of Mary. She was also jealous of Claire. She had good reason, for although Perce and Claire were only going for walks, Claire had set her cap

# a load of old ball crunchers

at him. (They didn't have the pill in those days.) Mary's uneasy feelings about Perce's relationship with Claire didn't stop her propositioning a friend of Perce's called Hogg. She was quite happy for Hogg to make up a *menage à trois*, but not keen to let Claire make it a *menage à quatre*. I wonder why our teachers never told us anything about this side of famous people's lives. There we were assuming

*Percy looking bored in Italy because ... can't find Mary. When I was in Italy, I found plenty, usually unasked for*

they sat at home sewing or reading or went to church and the whole lot of them were at it like rabbits.

Mary's child died at the age of nine days, thus not giving Perce the chance to wonder whether he could cope with anything else but the conceiving bit. Mary got pregnant again (the spill not the pill remember) and gave birth to a son, William.

Shelley was having money problems, so what better than an extended holiday to economise? Mary, Perce and Claire set themselves up at the Villa Diodati in Geneva, and this was where Mary got the idea for *Frankenstein*. Byron and his mate, Doctor Polidori, came to stay and they all sat up at night talking about scary things. One night, when Mary couldn't sleep, she had a vision of a 'hideous phantasm of a man' with 'yellow, watery, speculative eyes'. It's possible it was Shelley after a night on the piss and the laudanum, but that theory has never been speculated.

Shelley encouraged Mary to turn her vision into a novel. It became a great success, probably because lots of blokes could identify with it. Claire became pregnant by Byron. Byron was a right laddo, though, and had already gone off Claire. He did at least offer to bring up the child, but refused to have Claire live with him. This is all beginning to sound a bit like upper class East Enders isn't it? The fact is that, through the ages, posh people have been able to do what they like. The only reason the Tories don't like the majority of single mothers is because they can't quote a bit of Shelley or make a decent cup of Earl Grey.

Mary's sister Fanny committed suicide, possibly because of unrequited love for Perce. Good God, what did this man have? It would have to be some poem indeed to get me into the sack. Suicide was a social no-no – so the family told everyone she'd gone to Ireland and died of a cold. However, everyone got suspicious when no postcards with the Giant's Causeway arrived. Poor old Harriet went to Ireland and caught a cold too.

Shelley and Mary were devastated by this news and, wanting to show how sorry they were, got married. Must remember to have a wedding next time two people I know kill themselves.

Mary had another child, Clara, and all the gang went gallivanting around Italy and settled in a house near Lake Como. Mary and Perce were bickering a lot about domestic issues, the sad old practicalities of life creeping in. In Italy, Clara became seriously ill, whilst Perce maintained he had been poisoned by some cakes. (They always have to try and top it, don't they?) Perce still insisted they travel to Venice despite the fact that Clara was dying. The baby died in the boat as they arrived in Venice. Mary thought that the baby's death was Perce's fault. Well, why shouldn't she? It was.

# 'Must remember to have a wedding next time two people I know kill themselves'

She became very depressed but recovered with the birth of a new child. Meanwhile, Perce got out his atlas to see where they could go to kill it off. Just in case he succeeded, Mary had another child, a boy they named Percy Florence (poor little bugger), and they moved out to the coast. There wasn't much to do because Mary became pregnant again (God, what a chore this is getting). She miscarried this one, though. When a doctor couldn't be found, Perce made her sit in a bath of ice. Strangely it worked, which he hadn't expected, as being a poet doesn't exactly equip you in the gynaecological department. It just enables you to find a rhyme for it.

Perce loved sailing and went off up the coast one day. On the way back, he was caught in a terrible storm and all on board were drowned. Mary limped back to London and put everything into raising Percy Florence, thus ensuring another spoilt little bastard would grow up to piss women about.

# 35

## cleopatra

looks like Alma in *Coronation Street*. Well that's what people think because Amanda Barry played her in *Carry On Cleo*. Cleopatra was not particularly pretty, but she certainly had something that made men slap their todgers on the table. Cleopatra reigned between 51 BC and 30 BC and was the last of the pharaohs. This was because the Romans were building up their Empire and crunching everything in their path like a bull that's just spotted Chris De Burgh's wife.

Seeing city after city fall to the Romans, the Egyptian Royal family, the Ptolemies, decided to ally themselves with Rome, a pact that lasted for two centuries. Cleopatra's dad, Ptolemy XII, had to pay tribute to the Romans to keep them away from his kingdom.

Cleopatra and her brother argued about who was going to take over the throne of Egypt (unlike me and my brothers who used to argue about who was going to wash or wipe. A few flicks with a wet tea towel would have sorted him out I can tell you). In the middle of these arguments, Julius Caesar left Rome for Alexandra in 48 BC. During his stay in the palace there, Cleopatra decided she had better pay tribute to him. So, she gave him a gift – herself wrapped in a carpet. Indeed, it was a shag-pile, and from then on Cleopatra could count on

*Cleopatra could pick up Channel Four with her hat, some consolation I suppose for having just the one breast*

# a load of old ball crunchers

Caesar's support. Before you could say, 'Put it away Caesar', Ptolemy had been defeated and killed. (My brothers did get on my nerves a bit when I was a kid, but not quite enough to make me fancy the idea of sleeping with their worst mates in order to get them bumped off.)

In the summer of 47 BC, Cleopatra married her younger brother Ptolemy XIV. Now, I have said on quite a few occasions that I'm desperate for a husband, but I would choose spinsterhood rather than walk up the aisle with the bastard that grassed me up to Mum and Dad about the broken settee.

*On the set of the film, Burton tells Mother Theresa that one day all this fake suntan lotion will make her all wrinkly like a concertina. In the background, Kenny Dalglish nods in agreement*

# 'Before you could say, "Put it away Caesar", Ptolemy had been defeated'

Cleopatra wasn't too keen on incest either, because she embarked on a two-month trip with Caesar along the Nile. They really got stuck in and Cleopatra had a son whom she named Caesarion (although I think he came out in the usual way). Cleopatra and Caesarion then stayed in a palace in Rome built in their honour.

Caesar may have thought that no one in Rome had noticed that he was nomping someone with a pointy head-dress from Egypt, but they had. He even ignored a warning from a Barbara Woodhouse look-alike about the Ides of March. Consequently, he was murdered by a group of conspirators from the Senate. He had lifted the old toga once too often.

# 'Cleopatra had kept her mouth shut for a while (I don't know about her legs though during this time)'

Once Julius Caesar had been bumped off, Rome split into factions and eventually fell into the hands of Mark Antony (who sounds like he ran a hairdressing business on the side) and Octavian. Cleopatra had kept her mouth shut for a while (I don't know about her legs though during this time). However, eventually she decided she badly needed a perm and so went round to see Mark Antony. Naturally

# a load of old ball crunchers

*A woman with a snake staring at her knockers.*
*In the Ancient World, things were unfathomably*
*different*

enough, she felt obliged to pay tribute to him and ended up under his toga. The Romans were not happy. They called Cleopatra a sorceress and accused her of all sorts of evil. They didn't like the fact that Antony was giving Cleopatra parts of the empire as well as parts of his body and was not even charging her for a wash and blow dry.

The situation eventually reached boiling point and Octavian declared war on Cleopatra. They met at the Battle of Actium. Egypt got stuffed and this defeat was attributed to Cleopatra's cowardly early withdrawal from the scene. Oh, come on, she could have had a million things to do. Housework doesn't stop just for some poxy battle, lads. Octavian waited for a year and then claimed Egypt as a Roman province. He defeated Mark Antony in Alexandria and Mark Antony asked to be taken to Cleopatra. He died in her arms and was buried as a king.

# 'They didn't like the fact that Antony was giving Cleopatra parts of the empire as well as parts of his body'

Octavian entered Alexandria in 30 BC. Cleopatra was captured and taken to him. She tried to pay tribute but Octavian wasn't interested. The old magic had deserted her and Octavian refused to put out. Cleopatra, realising that her once successful method of bedding the powerful had failed, decided to kill herself. I think this is a bit extreme. If you're no longer attractive to men there are plenty of things to fill your time with. . . like crying.
(Only kidding.)

So, with a total lack of interest from any one-eyed trouser snake owners, Cleopatra decided to get a real snake in instead and made an asp bite her to kill herself. I can think of better ways to go. Drinking and an overdose would do me. I don't think I should throw myself off a tall building, because I might kill a few people once I'd got up a bit of speed. Apparently, if you throw a sandwich off the top of the Empire State Building it gathers enough speed to crack the pavement. I know, I saw one coming down once and tried to catch it.

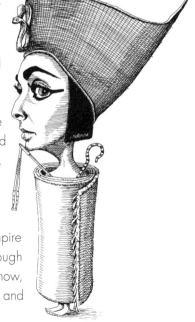

# livia

**livia** was in the fantastic *I Claudius* on telly. You might remember her as an evil old witch who bumped off anything with a pulse. Robert Graves, the author, used some poetic licence here. Yep, he made it up. It has never been proved that Livia, wife of the Emperor Augustus, actually did kill anyone. Still, she was a woman, so that's a good enough reason to slag her off isn't it chaps?

## 'Livia's husband obligingly divorced her, possibly with the incentive of being able to keep his body held together with his skin'

Livia married the Emperor to be, Augustus, in 38 BC. She was his third wife and was already married when Augustus met her. The slight problem of a husband has never stopped an Emperor ruled by his Y-fronts. Livia's husband obligingly divorced her, possibly with the incentive of being able to keep his body held together with his skin.

Tacitus, a Roman historian, reports that no one knows whether Livia was keen on marrying the Emperor. She was actually pregnant with her first husband's child, but Augustus was so desperate to get his mitts on her, he had her transferred to his gaff whilst she was about to go into labour. The child was called Julia and I call Augustus an impatient bastard.

Women in Roman times weren't given much respect. Two thousand years hasn't done a great deal for a lot of us has it? Roman women were ornamental and expected to stay in and look after the house. Men even went out and did the shopping but I doubt many of them actually came back with Bold Two-In-One washing powder, because men are a bit crap at shopping. It's always good fun to send them out for Tampax if you're bored (just make sure its 'Super').

# 'In ancient Rome, a minor nagging session could get you an introduction to Lenny the Lion and his big appetite'

At first, Livia won a reputation for generosity by making Augustus show clemency to his vanquished rivals. In Rome, once you'd beaten someone, you rubbed it in by pulling bits off them for a while before you finished them off. Women on the whole weren't quite as nasty. According to our mate, Tacitus:  'In domestic virtue Livia was of the old school, though her affability went further than was approved by women of the elder world'.

Obviously a lot of the old bags of Rome didn't have much else to do except drool over a bit of gore in between hoovering the stairs on their donkey-pulled Stannah stair lifts. Livia was very tolerant of Augustus's infidelities. One feels this may have been because she didn't have much choice. Wives of Emperors were particularly expendable in ancient Rome; a minor nagging session could get you an introduction to Lenny the Lion and his big appetite. (All right, I'm exaggerating a bit.)

# a load of old ball crunchers

Suetonious reported that: 'Augustus loved and esteemed Livia to the end without a rival'. Obviously crawling to old Emperor Shagbasket, there, Suet. In 16 BC, Augustus left Rome for Gaul, his secret aim being to live openly with his current mistress, Terentia. This was a bit contrary to his insistence on legislating to control public morals. This Roman attempt at Back To Basics was about as successful as Tory MPs' attempts to keep their hands off anyone marked 'secretary'. In fact, Augustus even exiled his own daughter and granddaughter to tiny islands, because they had committed adultery. At least it saved Livia the trouble of poisoning their lasagne.

Livia had called her son by the previous marriage, Tiberius. She was pretty keen for him to become Emperor. However, Augustus intended to settle the succession on several others, namely Marcellus, Gaius and Lucius. Lo and behold, they all dropped dead. Robert Graves's interpretation of the situation is that Livia wished to be made a goddess on her death and thought this could only be guaranteed

***When an outdoor disco in Rome opened called 'Heaven'
everyone went mad***

by her son. I've always thought Roman and Greek goddesses are a bit boring. I know you've got the Goddess of Love and the Goddess of the Hearth and all that, but what about the Goddess of Your Boyfriend Not Chucking You Just Before Your Birthday or the Goddess of Kebabs Without Those Horrible Gristly Bits In Them?

Marcellus, Gaius and Lucius could just as easily have been killed by good luck and disease. Lots of Roman Emperors employed food tasters to check whether food was poisoned or not. This wasn't totally foolproof, though, especially if you'd employed a food taster with a serious heart condition. People also got a bit suspicious if you had a day off sick.

*espite being the greatest Empire the world has ever known, Rome had en shittier mime artists than Covent arden*

Augustus did not like Tiberius and only adopted him when he had no options left. On the day of the adoption, Augustus pointedly added to the adoption papers, the words, 'This I do for reasons of state' – something the Queen might like to have written about the hats she wears at Ascot.

According to legend, when Augustus died in 4 AD, it was at the hand of Livia who feared that a rival to Tiberius, Agrippa Postumus, was to be recalled from exile and reinstated in favour. She smeared some figs with poison whilst they were still on the tree. Giving the food taster a day off, she ate those that had not been smeared, offering the poisoned figs to Augustus. The old git fell for it and he chomped away. According to Suetonius, Augustus died with her

# a load of old ball crunchers

name on his lips: 'Livia, live mindful of our marriage and fare well'. This may have lost something in the translation and he may have said: 'You old cow, I'll have you execu. . . .'

Tiberius wasn't even grateful to his mum for all her hard work. He attempted to ignore her as much as possible and, when she died, he pointedly ordered that she should not be deified. Livia's body was so putrid that Tiberius thought of entering her for the Eurovision Pong Contest, but he buried her instead. She wasn't too bothered at that point, though. I think the moral of this story is, don't poison loads of your husband's relatives on the strength of a vague promise from your son. I shall certainly think twice now.

# simone de beauvoir

simone de beauvoir was born in 1908 in Paris. Her father and mother were acting types, so her terrible temper tantrums were probably learnt from them. When she had these tantrums, her parents would put her in the broom cupboard. Not surprising then that she later developed feminist ideals, having looked at those instruments of female torture for hours.

As a child, she was also obsessed with religious ideas and would beat herself with a gold chain until she bled. This very quickly led her to decide that she didn't believe in God. It might have been a good

*arse jokes and free easy behaviour gust me..." No that'll er get published in ded'*

idea to not believe in her father any more, who very charmingly said to her when she was fourteen: 'My poor daughter, how ugly can you be?'. (A rhetorical question, I feel.)

However, Simone was very bright and did well at school and college. I do hope this cheered up her pig of a father. She started to teach literature in the poor quarter, through which she discovered the chasm that existed between the classes. This is also when her feminist feelings began to grow stronger. For example, her father believed that it was perfectly all right for married men to have a bit on the side, but not on for women to have the same freedom. But, as he believed it was all right to tell his daughter, at a most sensitive age, that she was ugly, he was king of the male chauvinist cochons.

# a load of old ball crunchers

At seventeen, Simone decided it was time she fell in love. It's all very well deciding to do that; finding someone to be on the receiving end is the problem. When I started off down that trail, I thought I'd set my sights low by looking for a man with a flaw, like a really stupid name for example. Simone struck up a friendship with Maurice Merleau-Ponty. She'd also made sure that she'd done better in exams than he had. Not surprising really that he had to stay in and wash his hair on pub quiz nights.

At this time in her life, Simone was a bit tight-arsed. She said: 'Coarse jokes, rude words, free and easy behaviour disgust me'. These are all the things that I like best. Simone completed a degree in philosophy at the Sorbonne in 1928 and decided to write a thesis on Leibnitz. With Jacques, a family friend, she started hanging around in bars, instead of going to the pictures. In these bars it was the tradition to dance with your partner without speaking a word. If you said anything, it meant you were a bit of an old slapper. However, after she'd got a couple of Snowballs down her throat, Simone began to change and said: 'There is within me, a yearning for the gutter'. I'm trying to identify with her here but, in these days of synthetic foodstuffs, I think I would have to say: 'There is within me, a yearning for the butter'.

Simone passed herself off as a Parisienne whore. This wasn't difficult when all you had to do was dance with someone and then start talking.

## 'Sartre was also experimenting with mescalin and for two days was pursued by a giant lobster'

***Michael Ignatieff practised boring famous people's tits off from an early age***

In her last year at the Sorbonne, Simone met three blokes from the École Normale Surperieure, one of whom was Jean-Paul Sartre. They were a rather aggressive mob who used to get up to wizard pranks like running around in the nude (Yawn). I had a male friend at college who streaked through the library wearing a balaclava for disguise. Afterwards, he asked a female friend of ours (who had seen it, but didn't know who it was) what she thought of his body. And she said: 'Oh, It was all right, but he had a very small penis'. The jolly trio nick-named Simone 'Castor', which is French for beaver. I don't know the French for 'tossers', else I would hazard a guess at her nick-names for them.

Simone and Sartre both passed their exams. They were becoming attracted to each other and he offered to take Simone under his wing. They became inseparable for a while. Sartre loved to spend money. He would flash it around at any opportunity he got. This may have made him seem rather attractive and generous until you realise he got all the dosh from his mum. He didn't buy clothes either and his mum and Simone were responsible for keeping him in pants and socks. Unfortunately, Simone couldn't keep him in his pants all the time, because he told her there was no way he could be monogamous. He suggested they stay close but have affairs on the side and always tell each other the truth. You may have noticed that, normally, blokes don't suggest this, they just get on and do it and bully for you if you catch them at it.

*'Psst! My neck's gone. Can you come and turn my head round'*

However, Simone agreed to have her cake and eat it as well, because in those days not many women were not getting the chance to stuff an éclair down. She became a teacher, but her Bohemian life-style did not impress the authorities. Sartre, meanwhile, was in Berlin and having an affair with the wife of one of his colleagues. Simone was a little *prise de panique* that he'd reneged on their agreement already and legged it over there. All was well, though. She was even introduced as his wife.

Sartre was also experimenting with mescalin and for two days was pursued by a giant lobster. He began having another affair, but Simone was relieved when she was introduced as his six-foot-tall jelly-fish. There were many situations in which Simone would take on attractive young female protégées and

Sartre would attempt to shag them. I somehow feel he was getting the better deal.

During the war, Sartre and Simone were working with Camus for the Resistance and Simone produced a novel. Sartre didn't produce anything except a lot of sperm. However, he was beginning to shape his ideas about philosophy and came up with Existentialism. Existentialism has about twelve million different definitions, but can simply be expressed by the phrase: 'Man is nothing other than that which he makes of himself'. Everyone was antagonistic towards Existentialism. Andre Gide, the writer, said: 'After the Great War, we had the dada movement and after the other Great War, there is the caca movement'. What a magnificent intellect! At this point, Simone really began to get going on her affairs. She met the American writer, George Algren, who was tall, blond and wild and they became lovers. He wanted someone to settle down with, though, so it didn't work out – because she kept going back to Sartre. Well, he didn't have any clean pants.

# 'As he got older, Sartre took loads of amphetamines. They weren't very good for his temper but he didn't half get round the shops quickly'

In 1949, Simone wrote her definitive work, *The Second Sex*. This was a colossal tome with many controversial ideas about feminism in it. Francois Mauriac, also a French writer, wrote to the publishers of the book to say: 'I've learnt all there is to know about your boss's vagina'. See, they don't mind us supplying it for their purposes, they just don't want us to talk about it.

# 'If you suggested to people that they conducted their relationships like Simone and Sartre they'd throw up their hands in despair'

From then on, Simone was portrayed as a *débauchée*, so she thought she might as well behave like one. She had an affair with Claud Lanzmann, who was seventeen years her junior, because he reminded her of a young Sartre. Why have the wrinkled old original when you can devour gorgeous young flesh?

Simone continued her writing and also visited Russia and China with Jean-Paul. As he got older, Sartre took loads of amphetamines. They     weren't

very good for his temper but he didn't half get round the shops quickly.

Eventually, Lanzmann buggered off and Simone realised she was getting old. I realised this when I got a cardigan for Christmas from my mum. . . and I thought it was quite nice.

Simone continued to support many causes including the student uprising in Paris in the sixties and pro-abortionists. They marched in Paris carrying parsley, the symbol of clandestine abortion (Eh?).

Simone and Sartre died six years apart from each other. Their romantic experiment lasted all through their lives. . . a lot more successful than most marriages. If you suggested to people that they conducted their relationships like Simone and Sartre they'd throw up their hands in despair. This just goes to show that a lot of people are stupid.

# bessie smith

was born in Chattanooga sometime in the 1890s. No one is quite sure of her date of birth. In those days racism was rife (unlike today of course) and nobody considered the birth of another black person worth recording. Bessie was one of seven children and her father died shortly after her birth. In those days poverty was a fact of life for most black people (unlike today of course).

Bessie's mother died when she was eight or nine and the choices that lay open to her were the same as the number of passengers that will use British Rail after privatisation: two. Bessie could either join a travelling show or look forward to a life of manual labour. Not a difficult choice. Minstrel shows and vaudeville acts had flourished since the 1860s and Bessie got an audition through her brother, Clarence, for a travelling show. There is myth that someone called Ma Rainey kidnapped Bessie and made her sing the blues, but this is not actually true; like the myth that Cher has parts of her original body left.

*Bessie watching an episode of* **Baywatch** *and thinking what anyone with a brain would think about it*

A certain producer called Irvin Miller sacked Bessie from his show because she did not meet his standards of beauty. Considering his show was called 'Glorifying The Brownskin Girl' and sounds like an early version of *The Black And White Minstrel Show*, I don't expect she was too disappointed at being 'too black'.

Bessie toured with several companies and kept working through the race riots after the war. Pub goers got a nasty shock in the 1920s with the introduction of the Prohibition Laws making booze illegal. Drinkers went underground, as opposed to lying on the ground, but they still got up to hear Bessie. Incidentally, Bessie had always preferred homemade booze which was called 'white lightning', probably because of its homicidal properties, so she could booze away to her heart's content.

Bessie married a guy called Earl Love, who died quite soon after the wedding, though not following a mega sesh on the white lightning, well, as far as I know. Bessie was becoming very popular at this point. The record industry was flourishing and black singers became popular – not because the industry had decided to become anti-racist, you understand, but because they realised they could make money out of black voices.

*e hat or the curtain*
*uld look ridiculous on*
*eir own; but as a*
*mbo . . . pure taste!*

Bessie was not the type to be exploited, though. She was a feisty woman who wouldn't take any nonsense. One day, whilst she was appearing in a show called *How Come*, the writer of the show bumped into her and Bessie let out a stream of obscene abuse. She was sacked. In those days you could find yourself without a job for the most trivial reasons; you may have noticed that the Tories have done their best to reinstate this.

Bessie was promiscuous. Nothing wrong with that, nomping comes a close second to stuffing your face – a phrase I'm thinking of using as my new motto. Bessie fell in love with someone called John Gee, a nightwatchman who was illiterate but who, for some reason, told people he was a policeman. (Not that that would have improved his chances of people taking him for an academic.) On the night of their first date, Jack was injured in a shooting incident, which I suppose beats, 'I was working late at the office'. Bessie moved in with Jack when he came out of hospital.

# 'In those days you could find yourself without a job for the most trivial reasons; you may have noticed that the Tories have done their best to reinstate this'

In 1923, Bessie made her first recording. Studios in those days weren't quite so sophisticated and performers had to sing into a big conical horn and keep going until it sounded right. Bryan Adams would have been in there until the end of time.

In June 1923, Bessie's first record was released and soon she was playing to packed audiences. Bessie shared all her money from her fame with her family. (My dad is living in a caravan. I guess I could buy him somewhere nice, but he wouldn't let me go out when I was fifteen, so bollocks to him.)

Despite the amazing talent of many black performers in the twenties, they did not mix with important people in the way white performers did. Black singers were never invited to go and meet the President. I expect the name of his house was enough to put them off.

At first, Bessie and Jack had a very happy relationship, probably spiced up for Bessie by her habit of partying until dawn and hopping in and out of the sack with a selection of blokes whenever Jack was not around. Anyone who messed around with her blokes was soon corrected with a fist sandwich. She wasn't scared of anyone except Jack. One night, at a party, Bessie was eating and drinking and trying to ignore a drunkard who kept asking her to dance. Eventually, she lost her temper and jumped on him and punched him in the head. (Must try that down my local disco.) As they were leaving the house three hours later, the same bloke jumped out and plunged a knife into Bessie. (Some blokes just can't take 'Piss off' for an answer.) Bessie chased the guy a long way and, eventually, admitted defeat. However, after treatment, she was back at work the next afternoon. Just chasing someone down the street would have meant a six-month convalescence for me.

As the novelty of fame wore off, Bessie's moods became erratic and she was drunk a lot of the time. Things were falling apart with Jack. Bessie legally adopted a six-year-old boy called Snooks and renamed him Jack Junior. At this point, she also started to have relationships with women. Jack was doing plenty of this, too, and when Bessie found out that he had messed around with another chorus girl, she beat the girl up and threw her off a train. Then she got hold of Jack's gun and shot at him, although people think she missed deliberately.

At that time, a phenomenon called 'the buffet flat' existed, which sounded fantastic to me until I found out you couldn't actually get a buffet there, but a selection of perverse sexual pleasures. Bessie was fascinated by an obese lady who performed an 'amazing trick' with a lighted fag. Although why stick it up your Auntie Mary when you could smoke it, I don't know. Another joy in America at that time was the reformed Ku Klux Klan, who dressed in white sheets and would have been laughable if they hadn't been so revoltingly evil. One night, Bessie was playing in a tent and the Klan started pulling out the tent pegs. (One of their more vicious attacks.) Bessie took some men outside with her and when they saw the Klan they ran away. Bessie faced them on her own, shouted obscenities at them and they legged it – well, as much as you can leg it when you're wearing a sheet.

## 'Drinkers went underground, as opposed to lying on the ground, but they still got up to hear Bessie'

Although Bessie was now loaded, she still preferred eating pigs feet and drinking bad liquor. Jack, meanwhile, was having an affair with someone called Gertie Saunders, giving Bessie good excuse to drive to his hotel and smash up his room. Bessie emerged from the room bleeding, but at least Jack chucked Gertie. Jack and Bessie split up soon afterwards and Bessie went out of her way to show him she could live without him, by living in another house I suppose. Bessie continued to make guerrilla attacks on Gertie and also went on to make a film and more records. She moved relatively easily from the Blues era into Swing, but was killed in a car crash after a collision with a lorry. If only she'd seen it coming she could have punched the driver first.

# madonna

is an icon. . . she even says so herself. The icon was born in Bay City in Michigan in 1958 and she was christened Madonna Louise Ciccone, although later she took the name Veronica as her confirmation name, which goes to show, you don't have any taste as a child.

Madonna's mum died when Madonna was five. Three years later, Madonna's dad, Sylvio, married the housekeeper, Joan Gustafson, thereby proving that if you do a bit of hoovering that's enough for

*idonna's shirt pops undone as e receives an award – an eration accomplished with ctronics and wires*

some men. Madonna remarks that at the time of her mother's death, no one really talked about the tragedy. This was, of course, in the age before most Americans discovered they could blah on *ad nauseam* to their analysts. Anyway, I won't blah on *ad nauseam* about Madonna's childhood because I think she's probably a more interesting adult.

Madonna was married for four years to Sean Penn, known in American parlance as a bit of a ' boy'. This is because he once pulled a face. Unfortunately it belonged to a photographer, and, once he'd pulled it, he punched it as well.

a load of old ball crunchers

Rumour has it that Madonna still wants Sean back, but he is now married with children.

**'Madonna was married for four years to Sean Penn, known in American parlance as a bit of a 'boy'. This is because he once pulled a face. Unfortunately it belonged to a photographer'**

Still, in America, marriages last roughly as long as the shipping forecast, so he might come back on the market again soon.

Madonna lives next door to Sylvester Stallone, so I bet going to borrow a cup of sugar is a marvellous experience. However, Madonna is one of those women who shrivels up and screams when she sees some sugar because it has calories in it.

**'Madonna has recently been given a white pit bull terrier puppy, so I don't suppose it will be long before her home is simple in a completely destroyed sort of way'**

Madonna has several homes, one of which was described by *Q Magazine* as: 'Simple in an expensive, yet unostentatious sort of a way'. Sounds a bit like Naomi Campbell to me. Madonna has recently been given a white pit bull terrier puppy, so I don't suppose it will be long before her home is simple in a completely destroyed sort of way. Madonna is someone who suffers multiple slaggings off in the Press. She believes she is being punished for being a single white female. I think she may be right and that the Press should lay off, but I do think someone should be punished for the film *Single White Female* which is absolutely atrocious.

*Not the most comfortable seat available in the new Habitat autumn collection*

Madonna has shocked a lot of people by wearing conical bras and simulating masturbation on stage. This is not such a big deal, you can see thousands of men doing it at football every week. (Obviously, I accept there aren't many wearing conical bras.) The problem is that lots of men can't cope with the idea of women masturbating. Surely that's why men were designed to go to sleep as soon as they've come – to give us women half a chance?

Madonna also gets slagged off by lots of women. The Courtney Love generation can't seem to find a good word to say about her. Madonna thinks this is unfair because she's 'opened the door for them'. Surely, that's a man's job?

Madonna is going to have a child. That old biological clock is ticking away and in your late thirties, the bongs get a lot louder. I'm at that age, too, and if I do have a baby I'm going to have a home

# a load of old ball crunchers

*Madonna is so successful, she can buy whatever she wants. Here she sports Mata Hari's neck, bought at a Dusseldorf auction*

birth. Not for any romantic reasons, just because I can't be bothered to get off the settee.

Whitney Houston has said that if any of her children turned out like Madonna, she would kill them. Nothing like a bit of sisterhood is there? Perhaps Whitney's worried the kid might show her up talent-wise.

Madonna does seem to be a target for misogyny, but that would be because she's a woman, and, let's face it, at one time or another we're all targets. I'm just a particularly easy one to hit.

I do think Madonna lets herself down on occasion. Her film *In Bed With Madonna* showed her praying before every show that all would be well. I'm sure she's got better things to do (God, that is). Also, in an interview with David Letterman, in an attempt to deflect back to him the numerous piss-takes they'd done about her on the show, she said 'Fuck' about a hundred times. If this worked, I'd have made hundreds of blokes cry, but, sadly, it doesn't.

Courtney Love called Madonna a vampire who would bleed her dry. Madonna said she thought this was very nasty, just before she flew off because it was getting light.

Madonna's *Sex* book which included a number of erotic photos of her also caused a stir because of its rudeness. Norman Mailer said it wasn't rude enough and that she should have included a beaver shot. Yep, Norman Mailer's the sort of desperate perv that would have to resort to shafting a beaver.

Madonna is currently starring in the film *Evita* as Eva Peron, who Andrew Lloyd Webber has singing 'Don't Cry For me Argentina'. Unfortunately for Madonna, most Argentines do not see her as an icon and certainly not their icon. It was thought that Argentina might really end up in tears when Madonna started filming there. Madonna didn't exactly help matters by trying to chuck several posh Argentines out of their gym so that she could work out without letting them see her wobbly bits.

Even though Madonna can be a bit barking at times (she jogs miles every day), I do think she has given women more licence to behave badly and that can only be a good thing. Unfortunately, she's kept a few thousand journalists in work, so I for one would appreciate it if she retired.

One journalist who met her described her as: 'Heart breakingly delicate as a bird embryo . . .'. What a load of bollocks! Still, Madonna's got some balls, let's hope she hangs on to them.

# pope joan

No-one is really sure whether Pope Joan ever existed or not but it would be great if she had, especially considering the attitude of the Catholic Church, who are about as keen on the ordination of women as the Queen is on Ann Summers parties. Joan is mentioned in *The Lives of The Popes*, so I think we can give her a mensh here. Also, a book does exist about the life of Pope Joan written by a Greek bloke in the nineteenth century who insists that his facts are right, so here we go. . .

> **'Looking after geese is not a particularly taxing job, I would imagine. You spend your day herding a load of silly creatures around, a bit like being a royal detective'**

Joan's father was a monk and her mother a goose girl who lived in ninth-century England. Looking after geese is not a particularly taxing job, I would imagine. You spend your day herding a load of silly creatures around, a bit like being a royal detective.

Joan's father went off to York one day and heard the Bish of York instructing the faithful to go and spread the word to all nations. Being a well-disciplined sort of guy, he said to his missus, 'Let's go and do it'. They left England and arrived on the German mainland, all set to pour the goodness of Christian virtues into the ears of the philistines.

Joan's dad spent eight years wandering about trying to get someone, anyone, to hear what he had to say. Unfortunately, nobody wanted to listen, and, rather than just ignoring him, they set on him and did him a fair bit of damage. He was beaten, stoned, burned, hanged and then thrown into the Rhine. Well, who knows, you might feel like an opportunity to practise your butterfly after all that.

## 'He was beaten, stoned, burned, hanged and then thrown into the Rhine. Well, who knows, you might feel like an opportunity to practise your butterfly after all that'

It didn't stop there though. Various tribes wanted to do him a bit more damage. The Frisians put out his right eye, the Longobards lopped off his ears, the Thuringians cut off his nose and the tribes from the Erlking forests killed his two children and chopped his knob off. Now that is what I would call a bad day at work. Somehow, nothing seemed enjoyable to poor old Dad any more. He knew he could not father any more children, although his wife stuck by him, or to him on occasions when his scars were a bit dodgy. To add insult to his multiple injuries, his wife was raped by two archers (no not two of The Archers) and nine months later gave birth to Joan. Poor old Joan, I don't expect being bounced on her dad's knee was a bundle of laughs.

Joan didn't fare much better as a young girl either. One night, some monks tried to rape her and, despite her hiding behind a tomb containing the bones of some saints, they were not dissuaded.

# a load of old ball crunchers

Eventually Joan tried to beat them off with a thigh bone of one of the aforementioned saints. Still they kept coming – or trying to. Eventually, as one of the monks was about to make a forced entry, Joan suddenly grew a huge beard that scared them to death and they all ran away. (I don't know about you, but I think this Greek author's taking the piss.)

Joan then met a Benedictine monk, Frumentius, with whom she fell in love. Either he was a big fan of bearded ladies, or she'd been to work with the Ladyshave. I'm not sure.

Joan and Fru decided to run away together and he persuaded her to dress as a male monk so they could share a cell together. Let's just review the situation. So far we have the daughter of a one-eyed, no-nosed, one-eared monk, shagging another monk, dressed as a man and with a beard that keeps popping up when there's danger. If only they'd had *This Is Your Life* in Joan's time, Michael Aspel would have had a riot.

*The first Mr Khomeini fails to get a fatwa going against Geoffrey Chaucer*

Fru and Joan ended up in Greece, until Joan got fed up with Fru. He had a terrible habit which was he never washed. If Freud was right and we're all searching for a father figure, Joan was in for a very long wait. One day Fru woke up and discovered Joan was gone. He ran towards the harbour and saw her disappearing into the distance. She was off to Rome. She'd heard there were a few one-eyed, no-nosed, one-eared bits of beefcake there.

When Joan got to Rome, still disguised as a man, she eventually met Pope Leo IV and, because all the men in Rome had smooth faces, no one suspected that 'Father John' was secretly a vagina owner. 'Father John' worked as Leo's personal secretary, being particularly careful not to read her horoscope when Leo was looking, and when Pope Leo became ill and died, Joan was elected as Pope John VIII.

People got a bit suspicious at the crowning of the new pope when his shoes kept falling off because they were too big and even more suspicious when snow fell in Rome and there were earthquakes in the vicinity. Added to this, it rained blood in a place called Bresse, which then had to be renamed Any-Liverpool-Pub-On-A-Friday-Night.

Pope Joan realised she hadn't had a good seeing-to for quite some time. Getting her oats presented something of a problem, though, because any lifting of the robes would reveal tell-tale signs of some very unpopish appendages. She employed a young lovely blonde boy called Florus and sneaked into his bedroom a few times to touch his hair. This got boring very quickly though and one night Florus woke up and gave the pope one. (How many people can say they've done that?)

*Pope Joan standing in front of a new, though somewhat impractical coat, made for her by Vivienne Westwood*

# a load of old ball crunchers

Following a few hot sessions of lurve, Joan started to have convulsions and locked herself away. There were great plagues in Rome and eventually Joan felt she should get out and demonstrate that everything was OK. As she dragged herself up to the papal throne, looking like Meatloaf after four days on an assault course, she collapsed and out popped a baby. Pope Joan managed to save her blushes by dying on the spot. As for whether she went to heaven or not – well, God would have had to have been in a very good mood that day.

# bette davis

was born Ruth Davis in 1908. Hers was not a happy family. Her father never paid her any attention, so he was no different from any of the other millions of fathers in America. Eventually, after many rows, Ruthie, Bette's mum, got fed up and walked out taking the kids with her.

## 'The film which shot her to stardom was called *The Man Who Played God*, based on the life of any bloke you care to name'

At the age of eleven, Bette had a rather scary Christmas experience and I don't mean *The Great Escape* was on TV yet again. For some reason, Bette was dressed up as Father Christmas and when she was nosing about trying to find her presents, she caught fire. Anyone who went to Brownies will know that the thing to do in this situation is to roll

*The Davis sneer was achieved by looking down the nose, half closing the eyes and keeping the head very still. Lots of people missed it because they assumed Bette was asleep*

someone in a carpet, so that at least you don't have to look at their hideous burns. This is exactly what those present did and Bette was extinguished.

A couple of years later, Bette was enrolled for acting lessons by her mum. Mothers do love to push you in that direction don't they? You don't hear of many mothers enrolling their daughters for fighting or drinking lessons. Bette's mum's business wasn't doing very well, so she suggested that Bette do a bit of nude modelling. I'd have told her to stuff it. However, Bette complied and whipped off her Father Christmas outfit. Eventually, she was signed up by Universal and the family moved to Hollywood. Hollywood is quite easy to find because there's a bloody great sign on the hillside for those who can't read maps very well.

# 'You don't hear of many mothers enrolling their daughters for fighting or drinking lessons'

Bette's first screen role was in a film called *The Flirt*, in which she had to play the virtuous sister of a spoiled rich girl. She actually wanted to play the spoiled rich girl, but that was a real-life part lined up for her in a few years time. The film which shot her to stardom was called *The Man Who Played God*, based on the life of any bloke you care to name.

Bette's first husband was called Ham Nelson, a man she had known for some time. When it came to the crunch, Bette was a bit dubious about marriage. Very wise. I've never understood those women who are prepared to maim others in order to catch the bride's bouquet at a wedding. Now, if the bride had to lob the cake. . . Bette and Ham's sex life was a bit of a disaster because they were both very naïve. Still, there are a finite number of orifices to try and eventually Ham found the right one and Bette got pregnant. She had an abortion because of her career and went on to play a Cockney waitress in *Of Human .Bondage*. Cracks in the marriage were already beginning to show. Ham had no interest in Bette's career. What hope is there for women who work in an abattoir if a rising film star can't retain her husband's interest?

Bette was fed up with Hollywood and bogged off to England. Sadly there wasn't a big sign saying 'England' so she was forced to go back to the States. At this point she met Errol 'Donkey Dong' Flynn who expended much effort trying to insert aforementioned piece of mammoth equipment into our Bette. In fact, he went to great lengths with his great length. Bette managed to resist the temptation of Errol Flynn, because she didn't just want to be another notch on his bedpost. One assumes his bedpost had the appearance of being seriously peppered with woodworm. Howard Hughes was a much more attractive prospect, and he and Bette got stuck into a very passionate affair. Ham found out about the affair and installed a secret tape recorder to catch them at it. He'd picked the right multi-millionaire to blackmail and made a packet.

Bette went on to make *The Private Lives of Elizabeth and Essex* with old Mr Desperate- For-A-Jump Flynn. Bette wanted neither his todger or his presence in the

*Bette is taken out for a slap-up meal of decorative toilet roll holders*

# a load of old ball crunchers

film, preferring Laurence Olivier. Flynn decided that if he couldn't have Bette, he would make her life a misery. He took the piss mercilessly about everything she did. Unfortunately she couldn't come back with the riposte of 'Mr Tiny'.

When Bette's marriage to Ham broke up she became very depressed. After her divorce from Ham she married a bloke called Arthur Farnsworth, but Arthur was an alcoholic so it didn't take long before that relationship was in trouble, too. World War Two broke out and Bette offered her services to the White House, who demurred on the grounds that an actress probably wouldn't be able to take on Hitler single-handed. Then Arthur Farnsworth died, mysteriously falling backwards outside a shop and cracking his skull, which is medically known as an occupational hazard of being a piss artist.

Bette was starting to get a reputation as a bit of a cow. On set one day, as she washed out her eyes, she shrieked with pain and it was discovered someone had put acetone in the bottle. Still, at least she could have got her nail varnish off with it, so it didn't go to waste.

At this point, Bette went on a bit of a nomping frenzy with a load of servicemen. When one of them was asked what the attraction was, he said, 'I've heard she screws like a mink'. How charming and sensitive.

Bette's third marriage was to William Sherry, ex-boxer, ex-Navy man and ex-husband fairly sharpish. The couple did have time to have a daughter called BD though. Her marriages were starting to last as long as an Italian government and things didn't go much better with the next husband, Gary Merrill, who was also a drunkard and violent.

All this may have contributed to Bette's inability to get on with anyone. Perhaps the best feud she had was with Joan Crawford, with whom she starred in *Whatever Happened To Baby Jane*. Do watch this because Bette's character reflects very well how I look on a good day. Joan Crawford put weights in her clothes so that it was a real struggle when Bette had to lift her up. Bette had the same struggle lifting her face up as she got older until she gave in and had surgery. She was disappointed with the results, as many women are. Save your money and spend it on fags and beer is my motto.

Bette died in 1989 with everyone quarrelling about whether she was really nice or really horrible. It doesn't really matter now, though, does it?

# martina navratilova has

suffered the slings and arrows of outrageous homophobia for many years now. For some reason, men don't like women being lesbians. Then again, men don't like women being anything so we won't worry too much about that. Marty was born in Czechoslovakia and, as a child, dressed like a boy and was often mistaken for one. One wonders whether as she grew up she felt like a man trapped in a woman's body. I wouldn't mind trapping a man in my body sometimes. I'll have to tone the old muscles up a bit more.

## 'I thought you only had one period and said to myself, "Sounds like a bad week, but I think I can cope". Wrong'

You may well wonder why I'm bothering to write about a sportswoman and yes, just the thought of sport does make me feel a bit queasy, but when I was a teenager, I was a bit of a dab hand at tennis. I once got quite a long way in the South of England schools mixed doubles championships, mainly because my partner had a very hard serve. I knew this because he served right into my bum on numerous occasions, arguing that it frequently caused an eclipse of the sun.

Martina arrived in Florida at the age of sixteen and was affected enormously by the difference between Florida and Czechoslovakia. She was particularly fascinated by the shop Seven-Eleven and how much you could buy in it. My local Seven-Eleven in South London does a passable impression of the bowels of hell after ten at night, so perhaps I should move to Czechoslovakia.

Martina was a contemporary of Chris Evert and, apparently, both girls were hugely shocked when their periods started, as were most girls of that era, myself included, because our parents didn't tell us

anything. All I knew about periods was what I got from a film at school which I completely misinterpreted. . . I thought you only had one period and said to myself, 'Sounds like a bad week, but I think I can cope'. Wrong.

Chris Evert's first memory of Martina was spotting 'a hideous fat girl, sucking a popsicle'. Martina was also wearing a very unattractive swimming costume and had strap marks showing where she had tanned unevenly, a crime punishable by death in Florida. Because Martina was a bit overweight, which in Florida means she could pinch 0.000001 of an inch, she was nick-named 'the great wide

*rtina's sky diving technique,*
*•ich consisted of replacing a*
*rachute with a tennis racquet,*
*•ays landed her very accurately*
*the court*

hope'. Hurrah for uproariously funny fat jokes.

At that time, women tennis players discovered that when they toured with the men, the geezers were getting paid eight times more. So they decided to strike out on their own tour, before the men needed new balls. Martina's debut season in 1973 was a success, but in 1974 she really got going. In the Italian Open she reached the final, where she was beaten by Chris Evert. She might have put Chris off a bit if only she'd worn the swimsuit. In September 1975, she defected to America and plunged straight into a frenzy of capitalist consumption. She bought jewellery and cars, but no new swimsuit as far as I know.

# 'No wonder the Americans are in such a mess, they don't half talk bollocks'

In 1976, Martina was beaten again by Chris Evert at Wimbledon. The British women competitors that year all fell over before they could get on the court. On a sporting superstars programme in the US, Martina met the golfer Sandra Haynie who took her under her wing. She wanted to turn Martina's bad temper into positive energy. No wonder the Americans are in such a mess, they don't half talk bollocks.

# 'She obviously wasn't aware that you don't throw guns either, you shoot them'

Chris Evert married John Lloyd, a British tennis player seeded twenty thousandth in the world, behind an old table and a worm. Chris took John's name as her married name, which was frowned on by feminists at the time. People thought she was being very conservative but some of her best friends were lesbians, although, more importantly, not one of them had an uneven tan.

*man in the crowd is dejected at his patent for the first pop-...paper baseball cap has been...jected*

In 1980, Martina won her first Wimbledon and started an affair with the writer Rita Mae Brown, well known for her book *Rubyfruit Jungle*, which I would have read if it hadn't had the word fruit in it. They bought a house together and then started being a bit silly with their money, buying caviar and not eating it. They just wanted to have a fridge which looked well stocked. Wish I'd known. . . I'd have had a root through their dustbins.

Martina's parents had moved to Texas and she bought them a house too. They were not happy about her sexuality. Her mother told her that her real father had committed suicide because of an unhappy love affair and that Martina would go that way if she didn't watch it. Sounds like his unhappy love affair was with Martina's mum, if she was that bloody insensitive. . .

The tabloids were up to their usual tricks, describing Gabriella Sabatini as 'The Beauty' and Martina as 'The Beast'. I'm sure they would have been more cruel, but they could only manage words of less than two syllables. Martina and Rita Mae split acrimoniously with a big fight. Rita Mae threw a gun at Martina as she got into the car, not realising it was loaded. She obviously wasn't aware that you don't throw guns either, you shoot them. Martina moved on to Judy Nelson who was a doctor's wife and a bit of a socialite. Her husband's bedside manner can't have been up to much. Their relationship lasted seven years.

Martina meanwhile was storming it through Wimbledon to equal Helen Wills Moody's record of eight singles titles. Despite the fact that age was creeping up on her Martina stayed at the top for a very long time. Things didn't work out with Judy though and they had a rather spectacular public 'divorce'. I rather naïvely used to think that if I could fancy women, my problems would be over, but gay friends I know have as many if not more hideously emotional nightmares. Martina is reckoned to have made twenty million out of tennis. How many swimsuits is that then?

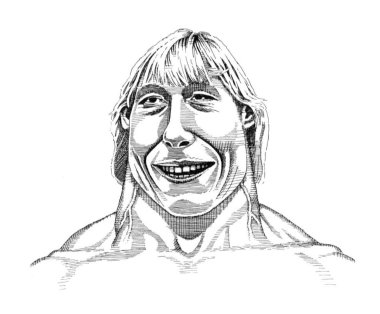

# joan of arc

**joan of arc** was not a fan of the barbecue, but she did have a tremendous effect on the course of history. Her intervention changed the direction of the Hundred Years War and I suppose there aren't many women you can say that about, apart from Margaret Thatcher who started the Falklands.

The Hundred Years War was between the Plantaganet kings of England and the House of Valois in France. Henry V was doing rather well after Agincourt (at least until he died and his infant son Henry VI took over) and things looked bad for the French. And then a seventeen-year-old girl from Lorraine appeared at the French court and introduced herself to the Dauphin Charles. Sounds a bit odd, doesn't it, just walking into the court like that? Still, Buckingham Palace is about as secure as a Wonderbra, so it is feasible.

Charles was in fact the uncrowned pretender and after the English victory at Agincourt, France was divided between Charlie and the Duke of Burgundy, who was a supporter of the English. After Joan's visit to Charlie, he perked right up. Joan explained that a voice from God had told her to raise arms against Orleans. In this day and age, an

*another bloke showing at an easy lay men are*

*Joan auditions for 'Medieval Gladiators' having chosen the name of 'Firelighter'*

immediate flurry of panic involving doctors, social workers and eventual forced admission to a psychiatric hospital would have been the result. Not so with Charlie. Joan persuaded him she was authentic by recounting a vision she had had of Charles, praying at the castle of Loches. I think I'd have asked for a bit more proof; like the lottery numbers or the name of my grandma's parrot. However, Charlie was up for it. His troops rallied and his fortunes began to improve.

The turning point came when the French defeated the English forces at Orleans in May 1429. Joan's charismatic presence is supposed to have aided the victory. Joan was very unusual for a woman of the time. She had a man's haircut and wore full soldier's gear. That she was accepted at all is miraculous.

# 'The English had been buggered by a teenage girl who should have been at home reading Smash Hits and weeping about the Take That split'

Joan's army attacked the fort in which the English were besieged and set fire to it by putting lots of faggots under the walls. What a terrible waste of a good dinner. The English soldiers jumped into the river Loire to escape the flames, or perhaps they were trying to get at the faggots because the French don't really eat them. The English had been buggered by a teenage girl who should have been at home reading *Smash Hits* and weeping about the Take That split.

# 'In these sorts of trials it didn't really matter what you said, they'd already made up their minds what they were going to do. It's the same these days'

Charles was crowned at Rheims with Joan at his side. After the coronation, Charles wanted to retreat back to the Loire. Joan wanted the French to press further north. Because she had won once, people placed their faith in Joan as she tried to storm Paris with the faggot approach. This time, it didn't work, but Joan was determined and had another bash at the Burgundians in Compiegne. However, she got it all wrong, her army was surrounded and Joan was captured. The Burgundians saw

*In order to appear more manly, Joan took lessons from a Monsieur Duncan de Norville*

# a load of old ball crunchers

Joan as a harlot and a witch, probably not because they thought she really was one, but it's a bit humiliating to be beaten by a woman and those were the best insults they could come up with.

Unfortunately for Joan, things went from bad to worse. She was sold to the English and tried as a heretic. In these sorts of trials it didn't really matter what you said, they'd already made up their minds what they were going to do. It's the same these days. If you wear a short skirt you want to get raped. Or for Joan, wearing army uniform and having a Peter Beardsley haircut meant she was asking to be ignited.

The trial was a bit confusing and Joan didn't even know what she was being tried for, so she couldn't really defend herself. Her 'voices' were used by the prosecution as grounds for heresy. If she was mentally ill, it's odds-on people would still have thought she was a witch, so she would have met a nasty end anyway. In those days, if you were an unusual woman, the locals had any number of reasons for dispatching you heavenwards. Just milking a cow wrong could ruin your chances of reaching a ripe old age, which, in those days, was about twenty anyway.

***Joan remonstrates with the Bay City Rollers, whom she is attempting to persuade to make a comeback***

Joan had been disowned by her own forces after her capture, so when the silly trial decided that she should be burned at the stake, there was no-one there with a watering-can to make her fate a bit more bearable. With such a terrible ordeal in store, one would imagine that it might just be too painful for people to countenance. Oh good Lord no. The medieval world was not like that. A burning at the stake was big time entertainment for the spectators, they were right up for it. Poor old Joan thankfully choked on the smoke, although all the spectators insisted on having a look at the body to prove that Joan wasn't some sort of witch who had flown off. People always suspect a woman of faking it, don't they?

Joan was posthumously acquitted in 1456, by which time it was a little too late for her to go back home, put a dress on and get on with the housework.

# judy garland

was really called Frances Gumm and her nickname was Baby Gumm. Her parents had actually wanted a boy, who they were going to call Frank, so not only did she arrive in the world lumbered with a dreadful surname, her Christian name wasn't that great either. Baby Gumm's dad was gay and she made her stage début at the age of two-and-a-half in a show called the *Kinky Kids Show*, so even the most amateur of psychologists could have predicted that this child was lined up for one or two problems in the emotional department.

*'This Head and Shoulders really works! I'll endorse it'*

Baby Gumm had the misfortune to plop into the world round about the time that Shirley Temple was at the height of her popularity, so immediately film studios started to trawl around for crumbsnatchers to push on to the screen so they could bounce around singing songs about lollipops and grow up to be completely fucked-up individuals. (Shirley Temple, on the other hand, grew up to be a US Ambassador. Enough said.)

Judy landed a seven-year film contract when she was thirteen. The studio was very impressed with her singing

*ly's fixed smile belies her
fusion as to why there is a
ge pile of cocaine covered in
wers on the table*

voice, but thought she was a bit too chubby. One would imagine that as responsible adults they sat down and worked out a healthy balanced diet for Chubby Gumm. But, of course, they didn't, they just forced a load of amphetamines down her throat. At the age of fifteen, Judy Garland was making two films at a time, studying and well on the way to becoming a speed freak.

Following the success of Disney's *Snow White*, the studio looked around for something similar and came up with *The Wizard of Oz*. At the end of the film, Judy didn't need to click the ruby slippers together, with the amount of speed she had inside her, she could have run back to Kansas in about five minutes. At this time, Judy worked a lot with 'child star' Mickey Rooney, who, although he looked like a teenager, was in fact about seventy.

# 'Judy didn't need to click the ruby slippers together, with the amount of speed she had inside her, she could have run back to Kansas in about five minutes'

# a load of old ball crunchers

Judy's first real romance was with an English-born musician, David Rose. They eloped to marry during a film, but the marriage was no bed of roses (more like a bed of Rose) because Judy was sexually much more mature than David. When she asked him to go down on her, he reacted in a horrified fashion. He obviously expected Judy to lie back and think of England even though she didn't come from here.

Not only did Judy have an amphetamine problem, she also found herself addicted to barbiturates, because on the amphetamines, she couldn't sleep. A bit pointless taking either really, like having a doughnut and then trying to counteract it with a Diet Coke. Judy was in such a mess by now that she was collapsing all over the place. David Rose got fed up with having to pick her up and they divorced. At that time in Hollywood there were loads of gay men around, including Tyrone Power with whom Judy had an affair. (Well, perhaps

they just talked a lot.) Judy met Vincente Minelli who was also gay and quite camp, but she was into the idea of marrying him so she could still have lots of flings.

Minelli and Garland married, much to the surprise of everyone in Hollywood, who were even more shocked when Judy retired for a bit to have a baby.

After the baby, however, Judy's health was starting to deteriorate even more. Eventually, the studio sent her to a sanatorium to recover from addiction, malnutrition and depression. In those days, her condition wasn't quite so hip as it is now. No Betty

*Judy forgets that Liza is now grown-up and can't be put to bed that easily*

Ford Clinic for Judy with a huge number of showbiz chums, just a Hattie Jaques-type matron and a couple of asthmatics. Judy separated from Minelli and on the set of *Annie Get Your Gun*, she only lasted a few minutes before she returned to her dressing room. Perhaps she had forgotten to get her gun.

# 'Judy also found herself addicted to barbiturates, because on the amphetamines, she couldn't sleep. A bit pointless taking either really, like having a doughnut and then trying to counteract it with a Diet Coke'

Her career at MGM was over. Still, her matrimonial career had a long way to go. She married Sid Luft, because she thought getting married again would sort out all her problems. That's a bit like thinking having an extra packet of fags a day will sort out your emphysema.

Judy had a second daughter, Lorna and suffered from post-natal depression, as well recognised in those days as quantum mechanics was in the Jurassic period. Despite the fact she was a big star, Judy also had terrible financial problems. She dealt with this in a very adult way by drinking loads. Eventually her body said, 'That's it, I've had enough' and fell over. In hospital in New York, doctors discovered

# a load of old ball crunchers

that both kidneys and her liver had swollen to four times their normal size. During her stay, forty pints of liquid were drained from her body. That's a lot of Scotch.

The marriage with Luft fell apart, followed by relationships with a Mark and a Mickey. Judy was falling apart all over the place. In Australia she was booed off the stage. People probably thought she wasn't pissed enough. In Hong Kong, she went into a coma. Then she asked herself to sing by her bedside and all was well. Judy ended up in Kensington and died of a drugs overdose. Makes you proud, doesn't it, to know such a big star died in our little ol' country.

# mama cass

**mama cass** had a supreme voice, but a very big body, so all through her life she didn't really appreciate the success and the talent she had because she was constantly made to feel unattractive by men. The only men that had sex with her were the ones who were after her money. Tragic, but better than being very fat and poor because she'd never have got a shag at all.

Cass Elliot grew up and out in Baltimore and in the early sixties she formed a band called the Big Three, which toured extensively on the coffee house and campus circuit. I've no doubt Cass had a few problems on the campus circuit given that students, in my experience, aren't the most tactful of audiences. Still, at least they're not very imaginative, either, and as most of them can only manage 'Fuck off, you fat cow', it's a wonder any of them ever get a degree.

## 'The only men that had sex with her were the ones who were after her money. Tragic, but better than being very fat and poor because she'd never have got a shag at all'

In 1964, Cass met Denny Doherty, a musician and friend of guitarist and songwriter John Phillips. With his wife, Michelle Phillips, John was touring the same circuit with his band, The New Journeymen. Phillips signed up Doherty for his new band, and Denny

*The photographer prays Mamma doesn't turn sideways or she'll disappear from the film*

then introduced John and Michelle to Cass. When John first saw her coming down the road, he said, 'What is that?' in the sensitive way that men do. The four of them took acid together and rolled around on the floor laughing. That's the trouble with people on drugs, they laugh at the slightest unfunny thing. That's why I like them all to come to my shows.

> # 'That's the trouble with people on drugs, they laugh at the slightest unfunny thing. That's why I like them all to come to my shows'

Cass really wanted to be involved in John and Michelle's band but they were dubious (I wonder why). She returned to Washington, but when John and Michelle went off to the Virgin Islands, Cass turned up again. She was dead keen on Denny, but he resisted. Some blokes just don't like the idea of fat women. Fair enough because we haven't got time to sleep with them all anyway. Cass was a bit of a wild one and would turn up with various drugs to experiment with. One day she produced a small glass vial filled with clear liquid and announced, 'One drop on your tongue and you're gone'. Yeah, gone to casualty probably.

# 'Unfortunately all people in California dream about now is money, making smoking illegal and how to lose that last 0.00007 of a kilo'

Cass and Michelle worked as waitresses for a time at a cafe used by lots of sailors. Cass was constantly insulted. They would shout, 'Hey fatty! You forgot our orders, or did you eat them yourself?'. I hope she did. The problem with people shouting abuse is that you always think of a witty riposte five minutes later, after you've kicked them in the goolies.

Eventually, John and Michelle let Cass into the band, although John reckons Cass made them look a bit ridiculous. (Not half as ridiculous as crushed velvet and cheesecloth made them look.) The band recorded 'California Dreaming' and Cass came up with the name, The Mamas and Papas. 'California Dreaming' became a big hit, although unfortunately all people in California dream about now is money, making smoking illegal and how to lose that last 0.00007 of a kilo.

The band did one of their first big gigs on acid and despite their fears the crowd really loved Cass, whom they saw as an earth mother type. Those fantasies were quickly dispelled when Cass

# a load of old ball crunchers

bought a Porsche. However, she was too big to get into it, so she bought an Aston Martin instead. Had she only had the foresight to purchase a bus, she would have looked really small in that.

By this time, The Mamas and Papas were superstars with a number one album and single. Consequently, they started meeting lots of other famous people. While in London, they met John Lennon and asked him for some grass, which Paul McCartney later turned up with. Unfortunately, it was real grass, so Paul had to send it to Linda to make a tasty veggie dish with.

The band also met Brian Jones and his girlfriend Anita Pallenberg, who had matching black eyes. He'd whacked her one, apparently, and she'd waited for him to go to sleep and whacked him one back with the phone. Bet that relationship was a bugger to sort out at marriage guidance. Cass had always been desperate to meet John Lennon and as she wan't there for the first encounter, the rest of the band persuaded John to go back with them and they tried to wake her up. Eventually, John managed to rouse her and they danced round the room although he came to regret moving to her country. When Cass foolishly started to experiment with heroin, she gave some to Denny and he threw up. Hopefully that put her off him a bit.

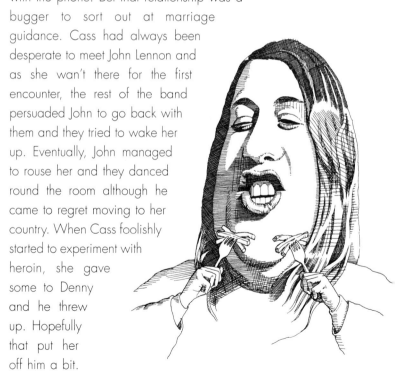

I always find a man chundering next to me to be somewhat of a turn-off, especially if it's because I've just asked him on a date.

Cass tended to be over generous to all the hangers on and there were many. Well, there was a lot to hang on to. She said it was easy to get a boyfriend. All she had to do was buy him a bike, a leather suit and enrol him in acting school. That's not the method I use. I sit on them . . . it's a lot cheaper. By 1966, the band had a second album out and were preparing to tour the US by jet. Cass was pregnant and she gave birth to a daughter, whom she called Owen for some strange reason . . . must have been the drugs. Cass eventually got fed up with the band and decided to go solo. By this time she was in a bit of a state as she had been fasting and had lost about seven stone in five months. She also had hepatitis and tonsillitis.

*God ... look at the state of her. Cass looks great though*

She married a friend, but it only lasted a year and her health started to go downhill. Poor old Cass died in London during a two week run at the Palladium. There were many rumours about how she died, the most popular being that she choked on a sandwich. A whole horse maybe, but not a poxy little sandwich. Doctors reckoned the fat round her heart had weakened it, but I prefer to believe it was the stress of the dieting.

# 46
# the rani lakshmi of jhansi

was born in Benares, the Holy City on the banks of the Ganges, in 1835. When she was still only fifteen-years-old, it was arranged for her to marry the Maharajah of Jhansi. This was supposed to be a great marriage for Lakshmi, although the Maharajah was twenty-five years older than she was, quite pudgy and a bit sweaty.

Lakshmi was prepared for her wedding by what was known as a bride decorator. Thankfully, this bride decorator didn't turn up four hours late with the crack of her bum out and drink tea all day. She was like a hairdresser, make-up artist and dresser all rolled into one. By the time she finished with Lakshmi, the poor girl felt so weighed down with all the paraphernalia she could hardly move. When Lakshmi complained, the decorator told her it had to be like that because she was a queen. So that's why Her Maj looks like she's got a poker up her jacksie then.

**'Lakshmi was prepared for her wedding by what was known as a bride decorator. Thankfully, this bride decorator didn't turn up four hours late with the crack of her bum out and drink tea all day'**

*e Royal Ballet limbers up on its world*
*r of the new production of*
*Massive Ruck'*

Lakshmi was worried she'd have to live like a caged animal, but everyone told her not to fuss and shoved a bowl of bones through the bars. At her wedding ceremony, the priest granted Lakshmi three wishes. She wished for her childhood friends to be with her, an elephant, and gave the third wish to her father. Bit wimpish, don't you think? I'd have really gone to town and selected Damon from Blur as a back-up husband, loads of fags and a Black Forest Gateau factory in my bedroom.

# 'Lakshmi was also very skilled with weapons and even trained her own women's fighting corps, something as unusual in India as no hippies'

Lakshmi's wedding night was a bit of a disaster. Her new husband passed out and lay on the bed smelling of stale wine and garlic. He finished this off with a concerto of belching as poor old Lakshmi lay on a cushion wishing she was a spinster. Unfortunately, the old tub

# a load of old ball crunchers

woke up, grabbed Lakshmi and ripped off her sari. Not a night to remember, I wouldn't have thought.

Lakshmi was really supposed to live in purdah behind a curtain like a good wife, but right from the kick-off, she sneaked out when she felt like it and went to the stables. Lakshmi was also very skilled with weapons and even trained her own women's fighting corps, something as unusual in India as no hippies.

Lakshmi did give birth to a son who died very soon after. She was a bit worried about what the Maharajah might think, but very conveniently he popped his clogs too. The local women were all quite disgusted with Lakshmi because she did not perform all the required mourning rituals. They thought she should have shaved her head. Understandable really, she didn't want to be mistaken for someone in the British Army. . .

Speaking of which the Indian Mutiny was on the go, as a result of the introduction of the new Enfield rifle. This could reload very quickly and sepoys (Indian soldiers under British control) were told to bite the tops off the cartridges, which were smeared with pig and cow fat. This instruction showed the British military to be about as sensitive as a *Sun* headline about Paula Yates, given the Hindus' respect for cows and the fact that the Muslims were unable to touch pork. The sepoys thought that it was a deliberate attempt to defile them, obviously not understanding how stupid the British Army were. Their loyalty flew out the window faster than a window cleaner with no pants on caught with a heavyweight boxer's wife.

# 'Eighty-five sepoys refused to load their rifles and, with their famous sensitivity and cultural eclecticism, the British soldiers chucked them in prison'

In 1857, at Meerut, eighty-five sepoys refused to load their rifles and, with their famous sensitivity and cultural eclecticism, the British soldiers chucked them in prison. Naturally, the remaining sepoys weren't happy and mutinied, killing British troops. Within a few days there was a full scale Anglo–Indian war on the go and skirmishes broke out in many different regions. This caused a backlash and suddenly most of the country was in turmoil.

Lakshmi, the Rani of Jhansi, who was now in command following her husband's death, was forced to defend Jhansi against the attack of Sir Hugh Ross as the British tried to re-establish supremacy. The British probably thought that, given she was a woman, they could just knock her back with a couple of well-aimed

*Nellie the Elephant wishes she hadn't packed her trunk and said goodbye to the circus*

# a load of old ball crunchers

***'Stop immediately or I'll shoot myself! (That's foxed 'em!)'***

cucumber sandwiches and the offer of some free eyeliner. It wasn't quite that easy.

Together with her rebel comrades, Lakshmi regrouped and did battle with Ross's British forces at Koonch. Despite the fact that they fought hard, Lakshmi's forces were forced to retreat to a fort, from which they were subsequently driven out. The rebels decided to head for a nearby city to try and enlist more support and it was near Gopalpur that Lakshmi made her last stand. Lakshmi was no delicate little flower. She was a good fighter and wielded a tulwar with the best of them. In case some of you think this is a tea-towel, it is in fact an Indian sword. Lakshmi managed to chop a few Hussars off their horses, but it was one of those very unfair situations where the British had loads of guns and she didn't. She was shot in the chest and lay dying on a haystack. This was quite handy from a funeral pyre point of view and when Lakshmi died the haystack was set on fire.

Lakshmi was a most unusual phenomenon for her day and age. To find a woman in that time and culture leading an army would be like a transvestite being in charge of the British Forces . . . openly that is. We all know they do it in their spare time.

# marilyn monroe

is the ultimate sex symbol of the twentieth century. She was gorgeous, loaded and famous – something lots of us aspire to. Was she happy though? Read on. . .

Thanks to Elton John, you probably know Marilyn's real name was Norma (not so glamorous then). Well, Norma Jean to be fair. Her mum was called Gladys, but Glad wasn't too glad to have Marilyn.

Gladys had a long history of depression. She had moved to Hollywood after a failed marriage and got a job in a film laboratory.

*Can someone get me two safety pins, I've had a bi-lateral accident*

She met and married someone called Martin Mortenson, but soon got bored with him. Ten months after she left Martin, she got pregnant with Norma Jean. Not a great start then for Marilyn.

It got worse, because as a child Norma Jean was in and out of care, although she did spend seven years with one family. When Norma Jean finally went back to her mum, Gladys was depressed again. At this point, Gladys's friend, Grace, tried to cheer up Norma Jean by saying things like, 'You're going to be a Star'. So things looked bright for a bit, but then it all went wrong again.

Grace married someone called Ervin Goddard, but it wasn't happy ever after because he didn't want Norma Jean around. She was taken to an orphanage and had to be content with Grace taking her out a lot. To cap it all, Goddard tried to force himself on Norma Jean. Not looking too good as far as the men in her life are concerned is it?

NJ moved in with her aunt and Gladys was transferred to a long-term asylum. At the age of eleven, NJ had man trouble again when she was assaulted by her thirteen-year-old cousin.

One problem that NJ suffered from all her life was painful periods. I wish I'd been able to sing her my song, 'Feminax and Nurofen are a Girl's Best Friend'. She had a history of gynaecological problems. So, not only were all her male role models a bunch of no-good shits, but her equipment was faulty too. Put these together and I imagine you'd have a pretty weird attitude towards sex.

# 'Wish I'd been able to sing her my song, "Feminax and Nurofen are a Girl's Best Friend"'

Norma Jean suddenly blossomed at the age of thirteen. Sorry, that sounds like a line from a biography of Barbara Cartland. What I mean, I suppose, is her chest grew. Consequently, boys, being the big lung fans they are, became very attracted to her. NJ loved the attention and played on it. At the age of sixteen she met Jim Dougherty to whom Grace proposed on her behalf. He agreed, even though NJ asked if she could marry him and not have sex. I don't think he agreed to that bit. She called him 'Daddy'. Bit dodgy really.

She couldn't cook. I can't either, because it's too annoying having to wait any time for food to travel to gob. Jim went off to work abroad and NJ got bored. By now, people started realising how beautiful she was, so she found something she could do and began getting photographed a lot. Jim didn't like this and pointed out that she couldn't have two careers, by which he meant he thought she should have kids. Norma Jean ignored this and joined an agency and began posing for ads in magazines. She once asked a photographer, 'Why do I have to wear a bathing costume for a toothpaste ad?'. (Out of the mouths of babes. . . in a *Wayne's World* sense anyway.)

Norma Jean was persuaded to dye her hair blonde, because as we know, blondes have more fun. (Not without a bottle of factor 47 sun lotion they don't.) When Jim came back after eighteen months, NJ had completely changed. She had mutinied and eventually they divorced.

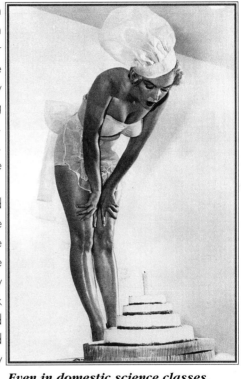

*Even in domestic science classes, Marilyn stood out from the crowd*

NJ then signed up with Fox and changed her name to Marilyn Monroe. She began to learn acting and picked up a series of no-good men who treated her like shite. What hope for the rest of us then! In 1949, Marilyn posed nude. This caused quite a stir (mainly in men's trousers).

# a load of old ball crunchers

Marilyn was very concerned about her looks and her biological clock. When she had an appendectomy, she left a note on her tummy, asking the doctor not to remove her ovaries.

She then met and dated Joe DiMaggio who was a very famous baseball player. Joe was a jealous man, and he had reason to be as Marilyn was already talking about marrying Arthur Miller (the writer). However, she did what Joe said to the point of agreeing to marry him. It seems that she was impressed by Joe's equipment. She said, 'Joe's biggest bat is not the one he uses on the field'. Why didn't she just say, 'He's got an enormous todger?'. Despite Joe's massive assets, their marriage lasted less than a year. After they split Joe's fans were very angry and Marilyn was handed a piece of toilet paper with 'whore' written on it. I'll let you guess which substance it was written in.

> ## 'She said, "Joe's biggest bat is not the one he uses on the field". Why didn't she just say, "He's got an enormous todger?"'

Marilyn began seeing Arthur Miller and, despite the eleven-year age gap – and the gap in their intellects, they married. Marilyn was now doing a film called *The Prince and the Showgirl* with Laurence Olivier. She drove him mad. Arthur wasn't too happy with her either and they parted after four-and-a-half years. By this time, it seemed Marilyn was driving everyone mad. On the set of *Some Like It Hot*, one three-word line took sixty-five takes. Some were too hot for comfort. But she had the power and the buggers just had to sit around and sweat.

Marilyn then starred in *Let's Make Love* with Yves Montand – and they did. When his wife found out, she was apparently very grown-up about it. Admirable. . . but very frustrating when you feel like going to work on the most beautiful face in the world with battery acid.

Much of Marilyn's wild reputation revolves round her alleged affairs with the Kennedys. Did she? Didn't she? I'm fairly sure she bedded them both. By now Marilyn spent most of her time in bed and was taking a selection of drugs and drinking a lot. A week before she died, her assistant reported she was in good spirits, by which she meant Marilyn had a lot of good spirits in her. Mystery surrounds her death and more theories abound on this than I've had hot dinners. Well almost. She was discovered in bed, clutching the phone, having died from an overdose. I know directory enquiries take a bit of a while to answer, but. . .

Anyway, so died the most beautiful woman this century, well, so people say, and if her end isn't a disincentive to the hordes of women obsessed with their appearance, I don't know what is.

# 48

**mae west** was born in Brooklyn in 1893. Her father was a boxer and her mum was obviously a bit nervous. Even though we all think people in those days went round being sexually ignorant and wearing white, the streets of Brooklyn were a bit of a hotbed, and Mae had her first sexual experience before her first period, in a basement with a dancing instructor. (An interesting approach to contraception, but not a long lasting one.)

Once her periods started Mae prevented pregnancy by inserting a water-filled sponge attached to a silk string. Always handy to have something to double up as a spare earring. At the age of seventeen,

*Mae doing her famous Lily Savage impression*

Mae married a twenty-one-year-old jazz dancer called Frank Wallace. He had to be careful, when he was practising his steps, not to slip over on all these sponges that seemed to be lying around.

Mae worked in Vaudeville and was quite a rude performer. She did a dance called 'The Muscle Dance' which involved wiggling suggestively on a chair. (I do this with a bloke sitting on the chair. I call that 'Park and Ride'.) The Muscle Dance ended with Mae's strap slipping down and one of her breasts popping out accidentally-on-purpose. Strangely enough, she was told to clean up her act or she would not make it big. Theatre at that time had fairly

*y Savage doing her famous*
*e West impression*

stringent rules such as no use of words like 'liar', 'slob' and 'son of a gun'. I must admit I was warned about my language once in a theatre in Llanelli by the manager and I'm afraid I couldn't resist going on in the second half and saying to the audience, 'The manager's asked me to stop using rude words . . . he's a bit of a wanker isn't he?'. (Actually, I said something worse than that but it wouldn't be printable.)

In 1926, Mae produced her own show, rather directly entitled *Sex*. She rented a theatre, hired a director, wrote and starred in the show, leaving just one job for someone selling popcorn. The show was about a Montreal prostitute and was panned by the critics so (natch) it became a big hit. Mae claimed that the word 'sex' had never appeared in the mass media before, except to define gender. This may have been a little optimistic, I'm sure there was a show in England called *Anyone For Sex, Oh No Sorry, I Forgot We're Victorians*.

## 'Mae claimed that the word 'sex' had never appeared in the mass media before, except to define gender.

# This may have been a little optimistic'

*Sex* was raided by the police and Mae was arrested by the vice squad who said her show was corrupting the morals of the youth (there was only the one youth in the audience), although they probably got her to run through it a few times just to check. Laws were passed for a year to close down any theatre showing dirty plays. Most people probably thought there was no point in going out, so they stayed in to watch telly which sadly didn't exist at that point.

# 'Diamond Lil became She Done Him Wrong, proving Paramount had lost all control in the grammar department'

Another of Mae's plays, *The Drag*, also caused uproar while still in rehearsal and Mae was given ten days in prison. Wonder if she tried to get someone to smuggle in a sponge hidden in a cake. Mae's next production, *Diamond Lil,* was a big success and gave her some respectability. She was obviously a bit bored with respectability, though, because *Pleasure Man*, her next offering, was raided by the rozzers again. I reckon the police just wanted another opportunity to stroke their truncheons. Mae was actually acquitted of the charges over *Pleasure Man* and due to her reduced rudeness she was signed up by Paramount. It is true that the less rudeness you use, the more likely you are to get an airing with a greater audience. If I toned down my act, I might be able to get on to BBC1 or ITV, but I don't fucking want to.

Paramount wanted a film version of *Diamond Lil*. Mae was offered a two month contract at five grand a week. She rued the loss of artistic control, but for five grand a week, she probably wasn't too bothered about losing anything. *Diamond Lil* became *She Done Him Wrong*, proving Paramount had lost all control in the grammar department.

Mae's next film *Klondike Annie* resulted in the newspaper mogul William Randolph Hearst laying into her. He decided first to lambast her and then ignore her, thinking this would be a good way to destroy her career. I wish Garry Bushell would get to the ignoring bit with me. Hearsty's campaign failed to prevent the film's success, proving that the public ignore the Press most of the time too. However, Paramount broke with Mae on the grounds that she was too low class and coarse. You see it's all right to be filthy as long as you say it in a posh voice.

# 'Mae was described as hanging around with "blacks, wrestlers and fags". Sounds great to me'

Mae was described as hanging around with 'blacks, wrestlers and fags'. Sounds great to me. After her dumping by Paramount, Universal offered her a co-starring role opposite WC Fields in *My Little Chickadee*. She had to take a wage cut and hated working with him. He would arrive every day with a flask of martinis and drink two bottles of gin. Must have been something else he did that was awful because that doesn't sound too bad to me.

In later life, Mae became a bit of a spritualist and explored her psychic powers. Most of us start to panic the nearer we get to snuffing it, quite understandably. Surely God must have a bullshit detector, though. Mae's career revived briefly in the seventies, but she died of a stroke in 1980. I'm sure she would have said that being stroked was a great way to go.

# 49

# dorothy parker

was fairly dotty. This may be because her mother died when she was young and she described her father as 'a monster'. If the young Dotty was late for dinner, he would hammer on her wrists with a spoon. At least he didn't use a hammer.

## 'Dotty said she only married him to change her name. (It was Rothschild . . . bit of a handicap to street cred.)'

Dotty grew up with a very jaded view of people. Although she was very polite on the outside, gradually she was growing very resentful on the inside. She would have made a good priest. However, the message she seemed to have got from the Bible was that if you're a truly good man you will be crucified'. I think ninety-nine percent of all the blokes in the world have got that message too. As far as Dotty's future was concerned, given the background she came from, she should just have sat on her arse and waited for Mr Right, a mythical creature who exists only in women's magazines and teenage girls' imaginations. Dotty couldn't wait though. She wanted to get a life. Dotty's writing career started when she had a poem accepted by *Vogue* magazine. She'd obviously got past that adolescent stage when you write lines like:

# a load of old ball crunchers

Oh, I love my Andy, I want him back, I am sad and my world is black.

Dotty was desperate to get away from her dad and moved into a boarding house. She supported herself by working in a dancing school at night and at *Vogue* in the day. Magazines were a little more intellectually challenging in those days. At the time, *Vanity Fair* published an article in French, because that's the sort of person they wanted reading the magazine. Well, I can really imagine that happening now. Unless the article repeated over and over phrases like 'Ou est la boucherie' and 'Je m'appelle . . .' they'd only have Eric Cantona reading it.

*Sadly, Dorothy Parker never turned her incisive wit towards her own fringe, which, in my opinion, is begging for it*

A Mr Nearly Right called Edwin Pond Parker came along and proposed to Dotty. He was a broker in Wall St and Dotty said she only married him to change her name. (It was Rothschild . . . bit of a handicap to street cred.) When World War One started, old Pondy Parker went off to work as an ambulanceman. Meanwhile, back at the ranch, Dotty and two male friends who worked at *Vogue* started having lunch at the Algonquin Hotel. Gradually, the numbers grew, until it became a regular venue for wags to go along to and say funny things. Dotty was the best at saying funny things, many of which have been quoted endlessly. My favourite one was as a result of Dotty being pestered by the editor of *Vogue* for an article. 'Tell him I'm too fucking busy or vice versa', she said.

I like this one because it's got swearing in it and I'm very childish. She also said, 'Men seldom make passes at girls who wear glasses'. Bollocks, men would make passes at badgers who wore glasses if they thought they were going to get a shag.

Pondy Parker came back from the war to find the Algonquin group well established. He tried his best, but he couldn't really keep up with them. His stories about bits of bodies he had picked up weren't really very amusing. Dotty was fired from *Vanity Fair* because some Broadway producers didn't like her reviews. Her two mates, Benchley and Sherwood, resigned in protest, so they had much more time to sit in the Algonquin and say funny things, but no money to buy dinner, sadly. Pondy Parker was sacked by Dotty and she fell in love with a geezer called Charles McArthur. He was a womaniser – as opposed to a woman who does this, who is not a maniser, but a right old slapper.

# 'He was a womaniser – as opposed to a woman who does this, who is not a maniser, but a right old slapper'

Dotty began selling her writing regularly to the *Saturday Evening Post*. It is interesting to note she had hardly any women friends. She was a man's woman. I find this strange. Normally if a woman has no female friends it's because she's got off with all her friends' boyfriends. I think it's very important to have women friends. You need someone to moan to about your bloke. You can't chat about your problems with another bloke. They just think, 'Great, she's vulnerable, I'll get in there'.

At one point, Dorothy said she wanted a little cottage with flowers, puppies and babies. This didn't seem likely as she was rather undomesticated. She used to eat raw bacon because she couldn't be bothered to cook it. I wish she'd written a recipe book – I'd have bought it.

Dotty got pregnant and had an abortion. (So much for the 'babies' bit then.) She also tried to commit suicide soon after and, when she came round in hospital, started wearing tuberose perfume because it is what undertakers use to mask the smell of corpses. (I thought that was disinfectant and sweat.) Dotty said she required three things of a man, that he was 'handsome, mindless and stupid'. It would have taken her a long time to work her way through the football league, though. She was also a secret softie. She romantically assumed that she would love a bullfight, but when she actually got to one, she got hysterical and ran out of the stadium. It does seem unfair that the bulls only get one proper chance to get their own back every year at Pamplona.

Dotty started having an affair with a young bloke called John McClain. He had a list of famous women he wanted to skewer on the end of his obviously tiny little penis. Poor old Dotty made the

***Dot, running the gamut of emotions from arse-holed to bored-shitless***

fatal mistake of falling in love with him and wouldn't leave him alone. At their final encounter he threw the words, 'You're a lousy lay'. This disqualified him big-time from ever having lunch at the Algonquin again.

In 1933, Dotty married Alan Campbell, who was a Broadway actor eleven years younger than she was. He sounds very good value though, because he did all the cooking and the tidying up. Can I have one please?

Dotty got involved in supporting the anti-Nazi league and also covered the Spanish Civil War, leading to suspicions later on in America that she was a filthy Commie. Then again, anyone in America at that time who had one tiny drop of the milk of human kindness was considered a filthy Commie. Dotty and Alan split, then got back together, then split, then got back together. This went on until one of them died . . . it was Alan. Dotty lasted to the age of seventy-three. Not bad for a suicidal, fag-smoking, hard-drinking dame. Something for me to aspire to, I think, although I've never been suicidal, apart from the time I ran out of fags in 1973.

# amelia earhart

I am not a fan of flying, so I find it very hard to identify with Amelia Earhart. If God had meant us to fly, he would have soaked us all in petrol and set fire to us. Amelia did not feel this way however, although there is nothing in her childhood which indicates why she was barmy enough to want to fly planes.

## 'If God had meant us to fly, he would have soaked us all in petrol and set fire to us'

Amelia was born in Kansas in 1897 and had a reasonably happy childhood until, in her teens, she discovered that her father was a bit of drunkard. The family called his alcoholism 'Dad's' sickness', probably because they were too polite to say, 'Dad's' rat-arsed again'. Amelia once discovered a bottle of whisky in her dad's suitcase as he was packing for a trip and poured it down the sink. Good job Amelia's dad wasn't a pilot really isn't it?

Amelia's family life was falling apart and, rather than falling apart herself, she decided to haul herself out of the mess and go to college, not something women would automatically think of in those days. Not these days either. Too many women are still convinced that they don't want further education because boys are more interesting. Can I just point out, at the ripe old age of thirty-eight, that they don't stay that interesting. Well, not like chocs anyway.

Towards the end of the First World War, Amelia worked as a nurses' aid doing such varied jobs as scrubbing floors and playing tennis with recovering patients. How horrendous . . . being made to play tennis.

Amelia's family moved to Los Angeles when she was twenty-three and she met a man called Sam Chapman. Together, they attended meetings of the socialist group, Industrial Workers of the World, or the IWW. Critics of the group said it meant 'I Won't Work'. Critics of the critics said it meant Irritating Whinging Wankers. At this point, Amelia went to see her first flying display and attempted to find out how much flying lessons cost. She had been bitten by the flying bug. Or bitten by some snake that had made her go silly and want to be thousands of feet above the earth.

# 'Amelia bought a plane for two grand. She had to ask her dad for the money. (Not quite the same as wanting a pony, is it?)'

Amelia looked high and low for a female flying instructor and found one called Neta Snook. Amelia had six month's worth of flying lessons although Neta was a little dubious about her ability. She must have been able to do it at least fairly well, otherwise she and Neta would have been a flaming pile of scorched flesh. To prove she was seriously interested in flying, Amelia bought a plane for two grand. She had to ask her dad for the money. (Not quite the same as wanting a pony, is it?) Her dad surprisingly agreed and she bought a plane called *The Canary*. (Yes . . . because it was yellow.)

# a load of old ball crunchers

By the age of twenty-five, Amelia was starting to attract media attention. She broke the women's altitude record and following a mention in the paper, one of her elderly relatives wrote to her mother to point out that 'the only time a woman's name should be in the papers is at her birth, her marriage and her funeral'. And, at the time, she would have liked to have bumped off the sexist toerag, I expect.

Amelia got engaged to Sam Chapman and her parents divorced. One might assume the former was discouraged by the latter, but no. Amelia became a social worker and looked set for a life of hard work, vilification in the press and being stuck to a hessian bag, when a phone call came through which was to change her life. No, she hadn't won the *Readers Digest* Prize Draw – she was being offered the opportunity to be the first woman to fly across the Atlantic.

Amelia kept it all very secret and told only Sam. Her parents found out through the newspapers and were very pissed off. It took twelve days before she could take off because of bad weather, bringing back happy memories to me of the now-defunct Dan Air. As this was a record-breaking flight for a mere woman, you might be surprised to find that Amelia didn't actually fly the plane at all. They were only going to let her have a go if conditions were OK. The pilot was hung over and the plane needed to taxi for three miles before it staggered into the air. I'd have given up and bogged off home at this point.

When the flight was under way, Amelia discovered the pilot had hidden a bottle of booze on board. No stewardesses with duty-frees in those days chaps. The plane landed in South Wales and news of the successful flight was flashed round the world. When interviewed, Amelia's father said he was disappointed she hadn't told him about her plans and that, in his opinion, she could do something far more useful than flying. Miserable old bastard. Amelia and crew went on to London where the two pilots who had actually flown the plane were virtually ignored whilst Amelia was lauded round London. She did at least feel bad about it though.

After this flight, Amelia became a bit of a heroine. She did a lecture tour, got a job as an air traffic controller, chucked her fiancé and married a man called George Putnam who had originally funded

# a load of old ball crunchers

her 'flight'. All these developments arose from just sitting in a plane for a while. All you get these days for that is a pair of swollen ankles.

Amelia, I have to say, did eventually come up with the goods and managed a successful flight across the Atlantic on her own. She landed in Ireland and having enough fuel left, considered the possibility of flying on to Croydon, but, as anyone who knows Croydon will applaud, changed her mind and didn't bother. Amelia held feminist views but denied she was a feminist. Probably because, even in those days, any feminist had to suffer the laddish tag of 'ugly lesbian who can't get a bloke'. The fact is, really, that any woman can get a bloke. Penises don't discriminate. Face it boys, not every woman wants a bloke.

Amelia decided to go for the big one and fly round the world. She flew across North Africa and across South Asia, but then it went horribly wrong. She set off to fly from Papua New Guinea to Howland Island in the Pacific and never arrived. Many theories abound, including the possibility that Amelia and her co-pilot were picked up by the Japanese. One thing is for sure; they were both completely knackered having had no sleep for twenty-four hours. I couldn't even drive my car down the road to get fags if I was that tired. Poor old Amelia was never seen again. Her concerns about her appearance, fat ankles and the gap in her teeth were the least of her worries now.